CHOOSE YOUR RETIREMENT

FIND THE RIGHT PATH TO YOUR NEW ADVENTURE

Emily Guy Birken

Author of *The 5 Years Before You Retire*

Avon, Massachusetts

Published by
Adams Media, a division of F+W Media, Inc.
57 Littlefield Street, Avon, MA 02322. U.S.A.
www.adamsmedia.com

ISBN 10: 1-4405-8655-1
ISBN 13: 978-1-4405-8655-2
eISBN 10: 1-4405-8656-X
eISBN 13: 978-1-4405-8656-9

Printed in the United States of America.

10 9 8 7 6 5 4 3 2 1

Library of Congress Cataloging-in-Publication Data

Birken, Emily Guy.
  Choose your retirement / Emily Guy Birken.
    pages cm
  Includes index.
  ISBN 978-1-4405-8655-2 (pb) -- ISBN 1-4405-8655-1 (pb) -- ISBN 978-1-4405-
8656-9 (ebook) -- ISBN 1-4405-8656-X (ebook)
  1. Retirement--Planning. 2. Retirement income--Planning. 3. Finance, Personal. I.
Title.
  HG179.B4893 2015
  332.024'014--dc23

2015008303

Cover image © almoond/123RF.

This book is available at quantity discounts for bulk purchases.
For information, please call 1-800-289-0963.

Contents

Acknowledgments 5

Introduction 7

PART I: Clearing Your Path to Retirement **11**

    Chapter 1: Your Money Psychology 13

    Chapter 2: Removing the Small Barriers 25

    Chapter 3: Demystifying Your Investments 37

    Chapter 4: Figure Out What You Want from Retirement 49

PART II: Debunking Retirement Myths **61**

    Chapter 5: Retirement Income Myths 63

    Chapter 6: Social Security Myths 73

    Chapter 7: Medicare and Healthcare Myths 85

PART III: Dream Big **101**

    Chapter 8: How to Retire in Place 103

    Chapter 9: How to Move Closer to Family in Retirement 127

    Chapter 10: How to Move Into a Retirement Community 137

    Chapter 11: How to Retire Abroad 147

    Chapter 12: How to Travel in Retirement 161

    Chapter 13: How to Retire Early 175

    Chapter 14: How to Change Careers in Retirement 195

    Chapter 15: How to Go Back to School in Retirement 205

    Chapter 16: How to Work Part-Time in Retirement 213

    Chapter 17: How to Leave a Legacy 221

Conclusion 235

Bibliography 237

Index 245

Dedication

As ever, this one is for you, Dad. I miss you.

Acknowledgments

This book could not have come to be without the help of many kind and knowledgeable friends and experts:

A big thank you to my editor, Peter Archer, who is unfailingly kind and patient, even when I am inconveniently overcome with the flu.

I am grateful to Dr. Daniel Crosby, who was kind enough to share his expertise with me.

Dr. Bradley Klontz took the time to answer my many questions about money scripts and provided this book with the money script quiz appearing in Chapter 1. Thank you for being so generous with your time and resources.

Thank you to Ramit Sethi of the website IWillTeachYouToBeRich.com for allowing me to use his excellent ideas on the importance of small barriers and how to use The Five Whys to overcome them.

Philip Taylor of PTMoney.com and David Ning of MoneyNing.com were both gracious enough to allow me to repurpose pieces I had written for them. Thank you both for being wonderful blogging clients and colleagues.

Thank you to every member of my family who listened to me read aloud from drafts in progress. I know it was boring. I know it felt like I was talking to myself. I promise it helped my process.

My sister Tracie is my favorite sounding board. Thanks for never being more than a phone call away through this whole process.

I'd like to thank my mother, Marian Berman, for cheering me on, for encouraging me to go on *The Today Show*, and for flying in at a moment's notice when I am inconveniently overcome with the flu.

My stepmother, Helen Guy, has been so supportive throughout my writing career and my unexpected career in finance. Thank you for all that you do.

And as always, I need to thank my husband, Jayme. This career of mine is exhilarating, non-traditional, frustrating, bewildering, and not a little weird, but I couldn't do it without you. I hope you know that I know that. Thank you.

Introduction

Whether you speak fluent NASDAQ or think an annuity is the French word for birthday, you have likely spent time beating yourself up for not adhering to the "right" path to retirement. After all, you know what you are supposed to do to have a secure retirement:

- Start saving for retirement in your twenties.
- Save enough to get your employer's matching contribution to your 401(k) each year.
- Maximize your contribution to your 401(k) or IRA each year.
- Be on track to replace 80 percent of your income in retirement.
- Save enough so you will have at least $1 million to retire on.
- Plan on minimizing your tax burden in retirement.

There are very few individuals who have followed every single one of these "right" steps to retirement. Even people who work in finance don't necessarily follow this path. (Full disclosure: I did not start saving for retirement until I was several years into my career, and I have only maximized my contribution to my retirement accounts about half the time since then.)

A lot of our fears about slipping off the retirement path come from the kind of financial advisers who delight in *coulda shoulda woulda* advice. If you listen to these experts, you might conclude that unless you can find a way to change past financial decisions, retirement is going to be out of your reach. For instance, you might hear a financial guru say:

"You didn't start saving until you were in your forties or fifties or later? Too bad! You should have started earlier to take advantage of compound interest."

or:

"You took money from your 401(k) and paid steep penalties? Too bad! You can never get back that lost wealth."

or even:

"You haven't made saving for retirement a priority until now? Too bad! You'll have to work forever since you didn't plan."

Despite the gloom-and-doom mindset of these experts, their idea that there is only one true path to retirement is dead wrong. In fact, each individual must find his or her own path to a secure and fulfilling retirement. That means you don't have to be perfect to construct a secure retirement for yourself. You can create a retirement path that fits your specific circumstances, rather than try to make your circumstances fit the "right" path.

And that's what this book is for. It will help you to determine what course you need to take to reach your retirement goals.

Choose Your Retirement

Reaching retirement is a highly individual process. Yes, there are some things that every worker needs to do: save money, plan ahead, prioritize goals. But depending on what you do for a living, how much money you make, how much you have already saved, what you want to do post-retirement, how much you plan to rely on entitlement programs, and what financial issues you struggle with, your retirement path will look different from anyone else's.

This book is broken into three parts that will teach you how to shape your retirement path—everything from determining the obstacles that are keeping you from maximizing your retirement savings, to examining the common retirement myths that might be holding you back, to showing you the path to ten different retirement scenarios.

PART I: CLEARING YOUR PATH TO RETIREMENT

This portion of the book will help you to identify obstacles that are keeping you from saving and planning for the retirement of your dreams. In Chapters 1 through 4, we will explore your money psychology and scripts, examine the mental and systemic hurdles in your path, determine your investment personality, and help you establish what is most important for your retirement experience.

PART II: DEBUNKING RETIREMENT MYTHS

The second portion of the book will help you to understand which common "facts" about retirement are nothing but myths. In Chapter 5, you will learn which retirement income rules of thumb are outdated, insufficient, or downright wrong. Chapters 6 and 7 will show you what you can reasonably expect from Social Security and Medicare in retirement. This section will allow you to base your plans for retirement on facts rather than conventional wisdom.

PART III: DREAM BIG

The final section of this book will show you the various paths to take in order to reach ten different types of retirement. Chapters 8 through 17 will walk you through the specific steps you will to take in order to achieve the retirement you want.

How to Use This Book

Parts I and II of this book cover information common to every retirement path, no matter which retirement dream you plan to follow in Part III. I suggest you read and work through those two sections before turning to Part III.

At that point, you can skip to the chapter or chapters in Part III that most interest you. Each of those chapters has the specific information you will need in order to make your retirement goal a reality.

Welcome to Your Retirement Path

Retirement planning can be overwhelming and confusing. There's no need to add to the stress by plodding through information that has nothing to do with your particular situation and plan. This book will help you cut through the noise and focus on the specific things you need to do to reach *your* retirement.

Let's begin the retirement adventure.

PART I

Clearing Your Path to Retirement

Before you decide what specific path you'd like to take in your retirement, we need to go over some basic concepts. If you've read other retirement books, including my *The 5 Years Before You Retire* (shameless plug!), you may be familiar with some of this material. However, it never hurts to go over it again.

CHAPTER 1

Your Money Psychology

WHAT YOU'LL LEARN IN THIS CHAPTER

Although there are many different paths to retirement, which one you take depends to a great extent on your attitude toward money. When you're done reading this chapter, you'll understand the four main ways people look at money, and you'll know which of these "money scripts" best fits you. As we proceed through the rest of the book's advice and exercises, you'll know how your feelings about money determine which retirement path works best for you. You'll also learn some basic exercises to begin building your self-discipline about spending and savings habits, which are key to a successful retirement path.

Most retirement books start by asking you to look at your current retirement portfolio and then do some calculations of how much money you already have saved versus how much you will need.

That is a valid way to start your retirement path. However, for most people, even the idea of looking up how much money is in their 401(k) is enough to touch off a nervous reaction. Even money nerds like me may find ourselves reorganizing our spice cabinet or calling to schedule that overdue root canal in order to avoid doing the minimal work necessary to start those calculations.

Why do we react this way? We want to be prepared for retirement, but the actual work of preparing seems overwhelming. We read books about retirement planning, but we leave the accompanying workbooks and worksheets uncompleted, the financial planners uncontacted, and the 401(k)s unfunded.

Understanding Your Money Scripts

You cannot separate money from how you feel about money. Trying to create a retirement path without recognizing that fact is a good way to create a path that your brain won't let you follow.

Instead of asking you to start by getting out your portfolios, I'm first going to ask you to dig a little deeper and think about your basic beliefs about money. These essential beliefs, which financial psychologist Dr. Bradley Klontz calls "money scripts," are usually unconscious. They are the stories about money that you have told yourself since childhood, and they are often rooted in how money was viewed in your family when you were growing up.

Money scripts can be helpful or harmful, but they will certainly have an effect on how you spend, save, and feel about money. Understanding your money scripts will put you in a better place to craft a retirement plan that will fit within those beliefs. It will be that much easier to stick to a plan that matches your psychological makeup.

The Four Types of Money Scripts

According to Dr. Klontz and his research partner Sonya Britt, money scripts fall into one of four categories:

1. Money Avoidance

2. Money Worship

3. Money Status

4. Money Vigilance

MONEY AVOIDANCE

Individuals with money avoidance scripts believe either that money is bad or that they do not deserve money. Common thinking in this category runs along the lines of *Most rich people do not deserve their money* or *Good people should not care about money.* These scripts are based upon the idea that money is a source of anxiety, fear, or disgust—and that living with less money is a virtue.

MONEY WORSHIP

Money worship can be seen as the opposite of money avoidance. It's based on the idea that money can lead to happiness and fulfillment. If you're part of this category, you may think *It is hard to be poor and happy* and *You can never be too rich.* The downside of money worship scripts is they can lead to things like workaholism, high credit card debt, or hoarding.

MONEY STATUS

If you're operating according to money status scripts, you conflate your net worth with self-worth. You might think *Success is measured by how much money I make* or *My possessions reflect my importance and worth.* Individuals with money status scripts will often be vulnerable to debt—because they feel the need to keep up appearances—and get-rich-quick schemes, since they want a shortcut to get that feeling of self-worth.

MONEY VIGILANCE

Money vigilance scripts tend to be helpful rather than harmful. If you think along the lines of these scripts, you probably think *Money should be saved, not spent* and *I have to research all purchases to make certain I get the best deal.* While these scripts can help your finances, if taken too far, they can have a negative effect on your psyche. For instance, following a money vigilance script can cause intense feelings of guilt when you spend money on yourself.

Working Through Money Guilt

I grew up with the money vigilance script that people should work for their money and not be given financial handouts—a script that I inherited from my father. When he passed away, leaving me as one of the beneficiaries of his life insurance policy, I felt guilty about receiving money that I did not earn, even though I knew intellectually Dad meant the money to be a gift. Being vigilant about money has mostly helped me to be money savvy, but it also caused me a great deal of unnecessary grief during an already difficult time.

WHAT MONEY SCRIPT DO YOU FOLLOW?

Once you know which money scripts most affect your financial behavior, you'll be in a better position to combat any self-destructive or poor choices those money scripts prompt you to make. The short version of the Klontz Money Script Inventory, which appears courtesy of Dr. Bradley Klontz, can help you determine which money scripts most shape your beliefs about money.

What's Your Money Script?

SCORING SCALE: 1-STRONGLY DISAGREE 2-DISAGREE 3-DISAGREE A LITTLE 4-AGREE A LITTLE 5-AGREE 6 STRONGLY AGREE			
Money Avoidance	**Money Worship**	**Money Status**	**Money Vigilance**
I do not deserve a lot of money when others have less than me.	More money will make you happier.	I will not buy something unless it is new (e.g., car, house)	It is important to save for a rainy day.
1 2 3 4 5 6	1 2 3 4 5 6	1 2 3 4 5 6	1 2 3 4 5 6
Rich people are greedy.	You can never have enough money.	Your self-worth equals your net worth.	You should always look for the best deal, even if it takes more time.
1 2 3 4 5 6	1 2 3 4 5 6	1 2 3 4 5 6	1 2 3 4 5 6

It is not okay to have more than you need.	Money would solve all my problems.	Poor people are lazy.	If you cannot pay cash for something, you should not buy it.
1 2 3 4 5 6	1 2 3 4 5 6	1 2 3 4 5 6	1 2 3 4 5 6
People get rich by taking advantage of others.	Money buys freedom.	If something is not considered the "best," it is not worth buying.	I would be a nervous wreck if I did not have an emergency fund.
1 2 3 4 5 6	1 2 3 4 5 6	1 2 3 4 5 6	1 2 3 4 5 6
YOUR SCORE:	**YOUR SCORE:**	**YOUR SCORE:**	**YOUR SCORE:**
If you scored a 9+ . . . *Money avoiders believe that money is bad or that they do not deserve it. They believe that wealthy people are greedy and corrupt, and that there is virtue in living with less money. Avoiders may sabotage their financial success or give money away in an unconscious effort to have as little as possible. Money avoidance is associated with ignoring bank statements, increased risk of overspending, financial enabling, financial dependence, hoarding, and having trouble sticking to a budget.*	**If you scored a 9+** . . . *At their core, money worshipers are convinced that the key to happiness and the solution to all of their problems is to have more money. At the same time, they believe that one can never have enough. Money worshipers are more likely to have lower income, lower net worth, and credit card debt. They are more likely to spend compulsively, hoard possessions, and put work ahead of family. They may give money to others even though they can't afford it, or be financially dependent on others.*	**If you scored a 9+** . . . *Money-status seekers see net worth and self-worth as synonymous. They pretend to have more money than they do, and as a result are at risk of overspending. They believe that if they live a virtuous life, the universe will take care of their needs. They tend to grow up in families with lower socioeconomic status. People with money-status beliefs are more likely to be compulsive spenders or gamblers, be dependent on others financially, and lie to their spouses about spending.*	**If you scored a 9+** . . . *Money-vigilant individuals are alert, watchful, and concerned about their financial welfare. They believe it is important to save and for people to work for their money—not be given handouts. They are less likely to buy on credit. They also have a tendency to be anxious and secretive about their financial status. While vigilance encourages saving and frugality, excessive wariness or anxiety could keep someone from enjoying the benefits and sense of security that money can provide.*

KNOW THYSELF

For many of you, the simple act of taking Dr. Klontz's money script quiz may be an eye-opening experience, because our beliefs surrounding money tend to reside outside of our awareness. Additionally, Dr. Klontz points out that we rarely have an opportunity to challenge our core financial beliefs, because money is considered a taboo subject in our culture, making us unlikely to talk about it. This is why discovering what your beliefs are about money and understanding that they are not universally true can help you change your behavior.

Dr. Klontz makes a further recommendation for dealing with harmful money scripts: trace them back to their origin. Often, you will find that a very entrenched money script has its origin in a traumatic event—possibly even one that occurred before you were born. In *The Journal of Financial Planning*, Dr. Klontz writes: "When money scripts are developed in response to an emotionally charged, dramatic, or traumatic personal, family, or cultural financial flashpoint, such as significant losses during the Great Depression, parental abandonment, or financial bailouts by a family member, money scripts can become resistant to change, even when they are self-destructive."

My Grandmother's Money Scripts

I can trace my script about working for my own money and refusing handouts back to my paternal grandmother, who grew up a poor farm girl in Kentucky during the Great Depression. She learned at a young age that she would have to rely on herself, and to be generally suspicious of both government and the wealthy. Even though I am generations away from subsistence farming in Kentucky, I still carry my grandmother's money scripts.

This is why it's a great idea to get to the bottom of the harmful money scripts you have been following. A very powerful tool for doing so is to interview your family members to determine what you learned about money in childhood. Not only will it help you to identify the specific events that may have led to your disordered money behavior, but it can also help you to clarify the beliefs you received in your childhood.

"You create your money beliefs in childhood, meaning the money scripts you learn are absorbed with a child's understanding and without any sort of balance," Dr. Klontz says. "Your parents may not have meant to give you an absolute money script. The money beliefs that are passed down to you could be qualified or amended from the absolute rule you absorbed as a child."

If your parents are still living, interview them about what they learned about money when they were children, about the important financial moments in your family's history, and about the lessons they intended to give you—and why. Even if your parents are deceased, interviewing siblings, cousins, and other relatives can still be very illuminating, tracing money scripts back to their source.

MONEY SCRIPTS AND YOUR RETIREMENT PATH

It should be obvious that someone with an entrenched money avoidance script will have just as difficult a time saving for retirement as an individual with a money status script—but for very different reasons. If you're a money avoider, you might feel unworthy of a large nest egg and find ways to self-sabotage your savings plans. For instance, you might give money away to needy relatives or charity. While there's nothing wrong with philanthropy, if engaging in it harms your financial situation, it's a disordered money behavior rather than an act of generosity.

On the other hand, the money-status seeker might have trouble saving money because she feels the need to impress others with her current spending—leaving nothing for nest-egg building.

Traditional retirement advice counsels both of these individuals to do the same thing: reduce expenditures in order to save more for retirement. At a basic level, this is right; that is certainly what both of those individuals need to do. But even though they have the same situation—not enough savings—they have very different psychological reasons for this condition and therefore have to approach the problem in different ways.

When it comes down to it, those psychological barriers amount to which temptations are likely to coax you away from doing what you really want: namely, preparing for retirement. That means the problem is an issue of self-discipline, no matter which money script you follow.

We'll talk further about how to handle the specific temptations and obstacles for each money script in the next chapter. But first, let's look at what you can do to improve your self-discipline, whether your temptation takes the form of a tricked-out sports car or an overgenerous donation to charity.

Understanding Self-Discipline

We tend to think that people with great self-discipline are born with stronger willpower than the average bear. For us mere mortals, it may seem as though the self-disciplined shrug off chocolate doughnuts and spending temptations with equal equanimity, never once tempted to stray from the path they have chosen for themselves.

As it turns out, while studies have found that there is a difference in the prefrontal cortex (the area of the brain associated with impulse control) between those who have impulsive tendencies and those with high self-discipline, the basic building blocks of self-discipline are learnable. In fact, recent research into self-control has shown that the key to saying no to temptations is to avoid them.

Time magazine reported on this research in 2013, stating that highly self-disciplined individuals "tend to avoid creating situations in which their goals would conflict, and reported fewer instances of having to choose between short-term pleasure and long-term pain." That is, staying true to your long-term goals is less about finding the willpower to resist temptations and more about setting up your life to avoid those temptations altogether.

This makes sense when you take into account the widely touted comparison of willpower to muscle strength. Just like a muscle, if you work your willpower too hard, you exhaust it. This is why a dieter might find himself ordering an entire pizza to eat solo on Friday night after a week of eating nothing but salad and lean protein, and a money saver might end up blowing a couple of hundred bucks on something she doesn't really want after saying no to smaller purchases for a month.

According to psychologist John Tierney, coauthor of the book *Willpower*, using willpower is a type of self-regulatory behavior, as is making decisions of any kind. Such self-regulation saps our mental energy in a process known as "ego depletion," which makes us weaker in the face of temptation.

It is possible to improve your willpower in the face of temptation. There are several tricks you can use to help self-regulate in the moment, even if you are coming from a long day of resisting temptations.

DISTRACT YOURSELF

In the late 1960s, psychologist Walter Mischel conducted research on willpower that has famously come to be known as the "Stanford marshmallow experiment." In this experiment, Mischel gave four- and five-year-old children a marshmallow or other treat, and told them they could have a second treat if they could hold off on eating the one in front of them for fifteen minutes. The children who were able to wait for the second marshmallow distracted themselves by hiding their eyes, singing songs, or pretending the marshmallow was a cloud.

Focusing your brain on something other than the temptation allows you the mental space necessary to ignore it. If you find yourself tempted to spend money that you really need to put aside for your retirement, start focusing on the reason why you're saving. Thinking about the retirement you want to have will help to motivate you to stay on track while giving your brain something other than the spending temptation to think about.

HAVE A SNACK

It turns out your mother was right: You do think better after you've had something to eat. Recent research by Matthew T. Gailliot and Roy F. Baumeister has shown that the ability to self-regulate depends on blood glucose levels. This is part of the reason why you may feel more alert and able to power through your to-do list right after lunch as opposed to right beforehand, and why it's so hard to stick to a grocery list if you're going shopping on an empty stomach. If you're feeling tempted by something you know you need to avoid, have a piece of fruit or another complex carbohydrate. It can help you get your willpower back on track.

REMEMBER YOUR MOTIVATION

Part of the reason why ego depletion is likely to make you give in to temptation is because it can reduce your motivation. Timothy Pychyl of *Psychology Today* explains this loss of motivation as a sense that success is too far away: "Given that depleted self-regulatory strength may leave us feeling like we won't succeed, 'we're too tired to try,' it may be that the reduced expectancy of success undermines our willingness to exert effort. It's not that we're so impaired that we can't respond. It's that we 'don't feel like it.'"

A great example of how motivation can change your ability to do something occurred on the day of the 2013 Boston Marathon bombing. On that day, many marathoners who had just finished up a 26.2 mile race decided to run an additional two miles to Massachusetts General Hospital in order to donate blood—even though under normal circumstances they would have been too exhausted after the race to run another step. They found the physical strength after the tragedy to keep running *and* donate blood, because their motivation was high.

It's easy to forget your motivation when it comes to retirement planning since the goal can either feel too far away to care about or too large to be able to make a dent in. There are several ways that you can keep your motivation front and center, including:

- Create an age-progressed picture of yourself. Researchers have found that you will feel more connected to and protective of your future self if you can see what you will look like when you reach retirement age. You can create such a picture at *http://faceretirement.merrilledge.com*.
- Post pictures of your dream retirement. We'll talk more about that dream retirement in Chapter 4.
- Imagine the worst-case scenario. Think through your biggest retirement fear and let yourself think about living through that possibility. That can be incredibly motivating.

Money: It's All in Your Head

No matter where you are in your retirement path, it can be both illuminating and effective to take the time to figure out why you do what you do with money, and to learn techniques to avoid the particular temptations that are likely to trip you up. As we continue through this first section of the book, we'll talk about more psychological and practical methods you can use to clear your path to the retirement of your dreams.

Chapter 1 Takeaways

1. To create an effective retirement path, you must determine how you feel about money.

2. There are four "money scripts": Money Avoidance, Money Worship, Money Status, and Money Vigilance. You've completed an exercise to help you determine which of these scripts is the one that runs inside your head.

3. To begin your retirement path, you must develop self-discipline about your spending and savings habits. How to most effectively do this depends on which of the money scripts describes you.

CHAPTER 2

Removing the Small Barriers

WHAT YOU'LL LEARN IN THIS CHAPTER

In Chapter 1 you learned about some of the big reasons people have trouble think-ing about money and retirement. This chapter will teach you how to remove smaller obstacles and get all your ducks in a row before tackling the big retirement issues of investment, savings, and healthcare costs.

Not all financial problems are deep-seated. Sometimes, what's keeping you from doing the things you want to do is pretty simple.

For instance, economists have long lamented the fact that poor fami-lies will often forgo filling out the paperwork for college financial aid for their children. These families are potentially leaving tens of thousands of dollars of financial aid on the table. One might conclude that either the parents don't care about education or they don't care about their children.

Nothing could be further from the truth.

The reason these families don't fill out financial aid paperwork is because *the forms are too complicated.* The Free Application for Federal Student Aid (FAFSA) clocks in at more than 100 questions regarding income, assets, and expenses. In fact, according to economist Judith Scott-Clayton, writing for the *New York Times*, the FAFSA "is longer and more complicated than the [IRS Form] 1040A and 1040EZ, the tax forms filed by a majority of taxpayers." Faced with a form that makes filing taxes look easy, the very families that most need financial help for college are the ones likely to procrastinate on the FAFSA until it's too late.

The amount of time necessary to hunt up financial information and fill out a boring and overwhelming form is a small barrier when compared to the amount of money available for low-income families who do complete the form—but it's a large enough barrier that it discourages a number of people from applying for aid and going to college altogether.

That is the problem with small barriers. They are generally surmountable, but only if you take the time and effort to identify them and leap over them. Until you get over your small barriers, you will avoid doing the simple and basic things that you *already know that you need to do* in order to prepare for retirement. The key to a secure retirement is taking the little steps toward saving and investing every day—no matter how many small barriers you may have in the way.

Small Barriers and Your Retirement Path

You might think that using the term "small barrier" is just another way of describing procrastination or laziness. However, you have probably personally experienced a small barrier within the past twenty-four hours—when you decided to wait to do something because a little thing was in the way.

If you have ever left dishes in the sink because the dishwasher needed to be unloaded, kept watching a TV show you weren't interested in because you couldn't find the remote, or let a cantaloupe rot in your refrigerator because you never cut it up, then you have fallen victim to a small barrier.

According to author Ramit Sethi, who coined the term "small barrier," there are two types of these barriers: active and passive. He describes each type on his blog *I Will Teach You To Be Rich*.

- **Active barriers** are physical things that keep you from doing what you want. For instance, the still-loaded dishwasher is a physical barrier keeping you from cleaning up your breakfast dishes, as are people who tell you that your idea will never work. These can be hard to identify, but easy to fix. Once you recognize them, you can make them go away (by unloading the dishwasher or ignoring negative people, for example).

- **Passive barriers** are things whose *absence* actually stops you from getting things done. Since passive barriers are things that don't exist, they make whatever you are trying to do much more difficult. A trivial example is not having a stapler at your desk. Imagine how many times a day that would get frustrating. (Apparently Milton from *Office Space* was right to be peeved about his red Swingline.)

According to Sethi, passive barriers are harder to recognize, since determining what you need is harder to figure out than determining what is in the way. That means they can be harder to fix.

According to *Harvard Magazine*, "In a typical American firm, it takes a new employee a median time of two to three *years* to enroll [in the company's retirement plan.]" For the most part, American employees are avoiding enrollment not because they are lazy, uninformed, or unmotivated. They drag their feet because enrolling in a 401(k) is complex and requires multiple decisions, each of which may require information or time that the employees feel they are lacking.

So how do you deal with the small barriers that are keeping you from your retirement planning goals? The first step is figuring out exactly what your particular barriers are.

THE FIVE WHYS

The world of engineering has created an excellent tool for determining the small barriers that are keeping you from your goals—particularly the difficult-to-identify passive barriers. This tool, which Sethi recommends using for personal finance problems, is called the Five Whys. It was originally developed by Sakichi Toyoda of the Toyota Motor Corporation in order to help diagnose the root causes of engineering problems. In the automotive world, a Five Whys technique might look like this example from Wikipedia:

Problem: The vehicle will not start.

- Why? The battery is dead. (First why.)
- Why? The alternator is not functioning. (Second why.)
- Why? The alternator belt has broken. (Third why.)
- Why? The alternator belt was well beyond its useful service life and not replaced. (Fourth why.)
- Why? The vehicle was not maintained according to the recommended service schedule. (Fifth why, and the root cause.)

While getting to the small barrier that is the root cause of your retirement planning hiccups can be a little less concrete than diagnosing the root cause of an engine failure, this activity can still help you to figure either what you are missing or what is standing in your way. Let's look at a couple of financial examples:

Problem: I decided to change my fund selection for my 401(k) last year, but I still haven't done it.

- Why? I don't know how to make the fund selection change.
- Why? I didn't go to the financial education seminar offered by my company that explained how to manage my 401(k).
- Why? I didn't want my coworkers to see me at the seminar.
- Why? I don't want them to know I need help with my finances.
- Why? It makes me feel stupid to admit that I don't understand finance.

In this example, the real barrier is feeling embarrassed for not understanding finance. Once you recognize that you are embarrassed about your lack of knowledge, you can tackle that problem—either by educating yourself or by asking for help from a trusted adviser. But without examining the root cause of your procrastination, you're liable to attribute it to laziness or weakness on your part, or simple lack of time. Knowing the exact small barrier that is keeping you from your goal means that you can face it head on.

Let's take another example:

Problem: I have not yet enrolled in my company's 401(k).

- Why? I haven't yet filled out the form.
- Why? I don't know my beneficiaries' Social Security numbers.
- Why? I don't have the kids' paperwork.
- Why? My ex-wife has it.
- Why? I am uncomfortable calling her for it.

In this example you may be all set to fill out the form to enroll in your 401(k), but you don't have the necessary information with you. So, you might put the form aside to deal with "later." But since you know you have to do something you don't want to do—namely, call your ex-wife— "later" never actually arrives. You end up procrastinating your way out of months or years of retirement savings, all because you did not want to make a five-minute phone call.

Once you reach the root cause of your procrastination, you may look back and think the small barrier that is stopping you is ridiculous. After all, no matter how uncomfortable a five-minute phone call to your ex might feel, or how embarrassing it might be to admit your ignorance about finances, neither of those things is actually going to hurt you. But these kinds of small barriers make up the two-to-three-year delay in Americans signing up for their company retirement plans.

Now it's your turn to identify the small barriers in your retirement path. An exercise Sethi recommends is to quickly list five things you would be doing to prepare for retirement if you were perfect. This list should focus on actions you would be taking (such as *Save 10 percent of my income*) rather than on the outcomes you would like (such as *Have $1 million in the bank*). For instance, you might list *Roll over my retirement accounts from the job I left four years ago* or *Make my will* or even *Downsize my house*. Quickly jot down the five things you wish you were doing to plan for retirement, but that you consistently procrastinate on.

Worksheet 2-1: What Would I Be Doing to Plan for Retirement If I Were Perfect?

1. ....

2. ....

3. ....

4. ....

5. ....

Now that you have identified the five things that you feel you ought to be doing to prepare for retirement, go through the Five Whys exercise for each one. By the time you reach the fifth why in each case, you'll probably reach the small barrier that is keeping you from doing the work you want to do to prepare for your golden years. Though the Five Whys exercise is presented to you in a single neat table, this will not be a quick process. You may find that you need to chew on your reasons for avoiding retirement planning and let the whys become clear over time. The important thing is that you start the process of identifying the root causes of your procrastination.

Worksheet 2-2: The Five Whys Times Five

Problem 1: ....

- Why? ....
- Why? ....
- Why? ....

- Why?..
- Why?..

Problem 2:...

- Why?..
- Why?..
- Why?..
- Why?..
- Why?..

Problem 3:...

- Why?..
- Why?..
- Why?..
- Why?..
- Why?..

Problem 4:...

- Why?..
- Why?..
- Why?..
- Why?..
- Why?..

Problem 5:...

- Why?..
- Why?..
- Why?..
- Why?..
- Why?..

Now that you have identified some of the small barriers that are keeping you from preparing for the retirement of your dreams, you're in a better position to deal with them and make your retirement planning much more productive.

In addition, recognizing small barriers can also give you another great tool for overcoming procrastination and other temptations. Specifically, you can use small barriers to outwit yourself.

Using Small Barriers to Your Advantage

One of the misconceptions about organized and productive people is that they are better at remembering things and more motivated to do the tasks none of us want to do. In fact, the born organized are generally just better at forcing themselves to do the things that they need to do—by using small barriers.

For instance, on days when you cannot forget the materials for an important presentation, you might place your car keys on top of your binder to make it impossible for you to forget it in the morning rush. You have created a passive barrier to leaving empty-handed. Similarly, if you're dieting, you might store Halloween candy purchased for trick-or-treaters in the trunk of your car until the festivities begin, meaning you'd have to walk all the way out to your car—an active barrier—to indulge.

Personal finance advice is full of little tricks like these that harness the power of small barriers to force you to behave.

Freezing Your Credit Card

One of the old chestnuts of financial advice is to freeze your credit card in a block of ice, so that it's impossible to make an impulse purchase on credit. While this advice may sound old-fashioned, it's actually a very astute use of a small barrier. The block of ice acts as an active barrier between you and a bad use of credit.

What's even more exciting than realizing that you can put small barriers to work for you is the fact that you can personalize the small barriers that will work best with your money scripts and temptations that we discussed in Chapter 1.

COMBAT MONEY AVOIDANCE SCRIPTS

Money avoiders tend to think they don't deserve to have money and feel as though their money would be put to better use by giving it away to charity or friends in need. The temptation to help others is what will lead an avoider away from saving for retirement. That means an avoider will need to create some small barriers between herself and her temptation to give:

1. Set up automatic transfers of your money to your retirement account. It's much more difficult to give away money that is already put aside for your retirement.

2. Unsubscribe from all charitable mailings. Go to DMAchoice.org and sign up for the Mail Preference Service program, specifying that you do not wish to receive commercial or charitable solicitations. (Be sure you specify both, otherwise you will only be removed from the list of for-profit organizations only.) You can also take a picture of the mail you wish to stop and send it to PaperKarma.com. They will contact the mailer for you. Also, you can use Unroll.me to unsubscribe from any e-mails you would prefer not to receive.

3. Tell family and friends who ask for money that they need to talk to you *and* your financial adviser. Many people have trouble saying no to family requests for money. If you commit to making financial decisions with the help of a trusted adviser, then you will have not only given yourself an ally in your retirement planning, but you will have added a small barrier to your family member's request. Often, making the act of asking for money slightly harder is enough to keep the moochers at bay.

COMBAT MONEY WORSHIP AND MONEY STATUS SCRIPTS

Money worshipers tend to feel that more money equals greater freedom, and they keenly feel that their lives would be better with more money. Money-status seekers follow similar scripts, in that they believe that success is defined by money and possessions. Those who follow either of these scripts are tempted by get-rich-quick schemes as well as overspending in an attempt to buy happiness. These individuals need to create small barriers between themselves and both poor investment decisions and poor spending decisions:

1. Institute a twenty-four-hour rule for financial decisions. Forcing yourself to wait until your excitement has cooled down will help you look rationally at a purchase that—in the moment—seems to solve all your problems. There are two ways to institute such a rule: agree to discuss all purchases over $50 (or $100) with your spouse, or get in the habit of only carrying cash when you leave the house.

2. Use a rubber band to wrap a folded-down 8½" × 11" sheet of paper around each one of your credit and debit cards. On the paper, write the following questions:

- Do I need to buy this?

- Do I need to buy it now?

- Will purchasing this item help me reach my goals?

- What else could I do with the money I spend?

Though the questions can help you to think through each purchase, the simple irritation of getting a full-sized sheet of paper unwrapped from around your method of payment can be enough of a small barrier to keep your buying in check.

3. Remove your credit card information from all of your favorite online retailers. When you can go from coveting an item to purchasing it with a single click, it is far too easy to spend money. Remove the "convenience" of having your credit card information stored, and you will give yourself a small barrier between you and mindless purchasing online.

COMBAT MONEY VIGILANCE SCRIPTS

In general, money vigilance scripts tend to help your finances rather than hurt them. However, money-vigilant individuals tend to be more anxious about their financial security, which can cause both psychological and financial problems. For instance, someone with a money vigilance script might be overwhelmed when an investment loses money and be tempted to cut his losses—when it is generally considered smartest to ride out market volatility (see Chapter 3 for more on this issue). An individual with this script needs to put one particular small barrier between himself and fear-based financial decisions:

1. If you know that you are likely to panic when you see the balance of your investments go down, only look at your investment summaries twice a year, which is more than sufficient to keep your accounts balanced. For all summaries that come in the mail, put a date on the outer envelope that represents when you can look at it—and don't touch it until then. For the accounts you can access online, choose an unusual password (but be sure you know your security questions) to keep yourself from checking too often.

What's in Your Way?

Whether we like to admit it or not, all of us have a tendency to drift through our decisions, reverting to habit and allowing minor obstacles keep us from our goals. But once you start looking at the world in terms of the small barriers that shape so many of our actions, you will be able to avoid unintentional barriers in your own life, and consciously mold your path to a secure retirement using the power of intentional barriers.

Chapter 2 Takeaways

1. Small barriers often stand in the way of large goals. You must identify these barriers and surmount them if you are to reach your retirement objectives.

2. There are two types of barriers: active and passive. In the case of retirement, most small barriers are passive.

3. You must analyze your barriers to find the problem at the root of each one so you can overcome it and move forward.

CHAPTER 3

Demystifying Your Investments

WHAT YOU'LL LEARN IN THIS CHAPTER

An important part of your retirement planning is managing your investments. This chapter will help to demystify the world of investing and allow you to feel confident about your investing choices. By the end of this chapter, you will know how to make the rational investment decisions—both during your career and after your retirement—that will best serve your needs. You will understand why it's a mistake to trust any financial guru who forecasts the performance of specific stocks. You will learn why doing nothing is a powerful tool in growing a nest egg, and you will be empowered to keep your money growing even after you are done saving.

Identifying and working on the reasons why you procrastinate on retirement planning—as we have just done in Chapters 1 and 2—is a great way to start down your path to retirement. Now you need an investment plan for all that money you've been able to put away.

Unfortunately, investments tend to be intimidating to even the most money-savvy layperson, and that can lead to some very bad decisions. Often, being stuck between the need to make investment decisions and the fear of making a poor choice is enough to paralyze you.

We're going to look at how you make your choices and why. Just as we began this book by looking at your attitude about money, in this chapter let's begin by discussing the emotions that drive most investment decisions.

Three Investment Vehicles

While there are a great number of alternative investments out there, such as real estate, futures, and FOREX, in this chapter I will only be focusing on the three investment vehicles you are most likely to encounter in a plain vanilla retirement account—stocks, bonds, and mutual funds.

- A stock is part ownership in a company. The value of the stock goes up when the company is showing a profit, and it goes down when the company takes a loss. A stock investor's general goal is to buy low and sell high—although some stocks also offer dividends. Stocks are by nature potentially risky, which means they are also potentially lucrative.
- A bond is an investment based on debt. When you purchase a bond, you have in effect loaned money to the issuing company, and you will receive interest payments in return, as well as repayment when the bond reaches maturity. Bonds tend to be relatively low-risk, which means their rate of return also tends to be lower.
- A mutual fund is a collection of stocks and bonds. It is likely that your 401(k) retirement account is largely made up of mutual funds. These funds allow investors to pool their money with a number of other investors in order to have access to professionally managed and diversified portfolios that they could not otherwise afford.

Investing and Emotion

Although this is a slight oversimplification, most experts agree that the boom-and-bust cycles that all markets see over the years are ultimately driven by two emotions: greed and fear.

For instance, in the 1990s, investors believed that Internet-related stocks were a sure thing—even when many Internet startups did not have sustainable business plans. (Remember Pets.com?)

Of course, the boom in dot-com businesses turned out to be a bubble, which burst painfully for everyone who had invested in them. This happened because investors listened to their emotional response to stock surges, rather than looking rationally at what the stocks should legitimately be worth based upon the underlying company's prospects. In the words of Federal Reserve chairman Alan Greenspan, investors were suffering from "irrational exuberance"—which is a polite euphemism for greed.

According to psychologist and behavioral finance expert Dr. Daniel Crosby, speaking at the 2014 Financial Blogger Conference (FinCon), feeling such exuberance is actually an excellent indicator that you're about to make a bad decision: "If you're excited about an investment, then it's probably a bad idea. Because excitement is not the affect [mood] under which you make your best decisions."

Just as the rush to invest in Internet businesses was buoyed by investors' irrational exuberance, the bursting of the dot-com bubble led investors to fear the market in general—despite the fact that when the market is at its lowest, that's objectively the *best* time to invest. As Warren Buffett famously stated in October 2008, "Be fearful when others are greedy, and be greedy when others are fearful."

WHEN NOT TO MAKE A DECISION

Why do our emotions lead us so very far astray when it comes to investing? It's partially due to something psychologists call an affect heuristic—a kind of universal mental shortcut in which you use your current emotional state in order to make a decision. For instance, Dr. Crosby states that clinical psychologists are taught to tell their patients not to make any important decisions about their life or their money when they are hungry, angry, lonely, or tired, because it is next to impossible to make a rational decision in those emotional states. Think of the last time you tried to make an important decision while you were feeling any of those emotions or states. It's likely that decision wasn't one of your best.

More generally, the affect heuristic means that when you have a largely positive feeling about something (like excitement about a new technology), this makes you more likely to perceive the risks as low and the benefits as high. On the other hand, if your feelings are negative (like fearing a repeat of a market crash), then you will likely judge the risks to be high and the benefits to be low.

How to Be a Rational Investor

How do you combat the negative effects of emotions on your investments? You may know what you need to do rationally, but it can be very difficult to resist the siren song of a "sure thing." It can be even harder to take what feels like an enormous risk with your money after a market correction.

According to Jeff Olson, author of the book *The Slight Edge*, the trick is to emulate Lady Justice, who is often shown blindfolded and holding scales: "The blindfold doesn't imply that justice is 'blind,' as people sometimes assume; its point is that true justice is impervious to external influence."

As investors, we can all find ways to "blindfold" ourselves in order to stay true to our investment goals and avoid both greedy and fearful distractions. In fact, Dr. Daniel Crosby suggests three specific ways to minimize the effect of external influence: understanding and calculating true risk, distrusting market forecasting, and doing nothing.

DO YOU KNOW WHAT YOUR RISK IS?

When most retirement books talk about risk, they are referring specifically to the volatility of an investment. Stocks are considered riskier than other investments because their value fluctuates—and using the word *risk* in this way is a shorthand description of the difference in volatility between stocks and other types of investments, such as bonds.

However, according to Dr. Crosby, the problem with defining risk only in terms of volatility is that it ignores two important truths about risk:

1. Risk is an absolute loss of capital. We tend to forget that money loses value over time because of inflation. That means keeping your nest egg in conservative investments such as CDs, Treasury bills, and savings accounts for fear of losing your shirt in the stock market is one of the riskiest things you can do with your money. Yes, your principal will be protected, but the buying power of your money will be eaten away by inflation. So when assessing the risk of an investment, you need to look at your risk in absolute terms, not just in terms of the specific investment.

2. Risk is individual and idiosyncratic. Are you the type who is ready to stash your nest egg in your mattress if the market takes a dip? Or are you more likely to chase dreams of riches from one investment to another? Depending on what type of investor you are, your absolute risk will be different.

A Chicken Little type who fears loss of principal will face the risk of not investing in enough volatile assets to get the kind of growth he needs to meet his goals. On the other hand, a starry-eyed dreamer who believes she can make an immense fortune quickly faces the risk of having too much money invested in volatile assets—and possibly losing everything. In each case, the potential absolute loss of capital comes from two different choices, each one stemming from the personality and emotional makeup of the investor. If you know how you are personally at risk of losing capital, you're in a better position to craft a rational investment strategy.

It's likely that you will take a risk-tolerance assessment at some point on your path to retirement. Often, advisers will use the results of such a quiz to suggest asset allocations that fit your risk tolerance. If you fall within the middle of the road in terms of risk tolerance, this can be a good idea. But if you tend to be either very fearful or very speculative with investments, then you might want to think about what your risk tolerance is costing you.

FORECASTING IS FOR WEATHERMEN

You might remember the brouhaha back in 2008 when CNBC's Jim Cramer told viewers that Bear Stearns was not in trouble a mere three days before the bank's stock fell 92 percent. To be fair to Cramer, he claims that he was simply stating that a viewer's deposit in a brokerage account at Bear Stearns was safe, and he was not making a recommendation to buy Bear Stearns stock.

Hair-splitting aside, there is no denying that Cramer ended up with egg on his face after Bear Stearns failed. How could a professional market prognosticator get it so wrong?

According to psychologist Philip Tetlock, none of us should be surprised when an expert like Cramer is wrong, because oddly enough, "the better known and more frequently quoted [experts] are, the less reliable their guesses about the future are likely to be."

This sounds ridiculous until you examine the role of media in experts' predictions. First, the experts who manage to make it onto a national stage are the ones who have built a reputation, which they want to hold on to. They will likely play up any prediction they have made that came true, and gloss over any mistakes. In addition, because it's very boring to watch an expert who states, "the market will fluctuate" (as J.P. Morgan once famously predicted), the brash experts with bold predictions make for better television.

No one can know with complete certainty what the market will do, but statistical analysis can give you a basic idea of what to expect. It's just not nearly as interesting as an expert shouting at you about specific investments.

Index Funds

You can use statistics to your advantage by investing in index funds. These funds aim to replicate the movement of specific securities in a target index. That means that an index fund is going to do about as well as the target securities will do.

Over the past twenty years, the stock market as a whole has seen an 8.21 percent return per year on average, despite two recessions. However, according to Dr. Crosby, the average investor has only gotten 4.25 percent return per year over that time. However, index funds have averaged a 6 percent return per year since the early nineties—beating out the average investor's return.

In addition, because the specific composition of an index fund is a known quantity, the fees for holding such a fund are lower than those of an actively managed mutual fund, so an investor who is averaging that 6 percent return is seeing less of that return eaten up by fees.

As Dr. Crosby puts it, forecasting is for weathermen. Watching expert predictions on television may be entertaining, but it's much smarter to go with statistical likelihoods for your own retirement fund.

DO LESS THAN YOU THINK YOU SHOULD

Back before GPS devices were invented, I used to regularly panic while driving to a new place if I stayed on the same road for too long—even if that was exactly what my directions told me to do. I had a tendency to worry that I was going the wrong way if I wasn't actively making turns or merging onto new roads.

That feeling of panic is a familiar one to many investors. It's common for us to feel as if we need to take an active part protecting our investments if things seem to be going poorly—even though we may know that statistically our money is in the best possible investments.

What's going on in both of those cases is called the "action bias," and it kicks in when there appears to be uncertainty or a problem. In the face of an ambiguous situation, our universal preference is to do something—anything! According to researcher David Wilkinson on the blog *Ambiguity Advantage*, "We are happier doing *anything*, even if it is counterproductive—rather than doing nothing, even if doing nothing is the best course of action."

Sitting tight on your investments is by far the smartest way to grow your money. According to research by Nobel laureate William Sharpe, you would have to be correct about timing the market (that is, buying stock at its lowest and selling it at its highest) 82 percent of the time in order to match the returns you will get if you buy and hold your investments over a period of decades. To put that in context, Dr. Crosby notes that Warren Buffett aims for accurate market timing about two-thirds of the time.

The reason why we are all so hesitant to follow a buy-and-hold strategy and why we fall for the action bias is because it flies in the face of what we know to be true elsewhere in our lives, according to Dr. Crosby: "Imagine if I told you that in order to lose twenty pounds, you should do absolutely nothing. The disbelief you would feel hearing that advice is similar to what you feel about following a buy-and-hold strategy—and yet, buy-and-hold is a time when you should do less than you think you should."

Doing less than you think you should when it comes to your investments can be particularly tough when it comes to retirement planning, since you likely need to be *saving* more than you think you should (or at least as much as you can). Once you've done the hard work of setting your money aside, it can be difficult to let it follow the vagaries of the market and just trust that it will grow without your input. As long as you have chosen an investment strategy that fits your needs and timing, keep your hands off of it for the long haul (other than regular rebalancing, which I'll discuss in the next section).

The author of *Pooh's Little Instruction Book* actually may have said it best: Don't underestimate the value of Doing Nothing.

REBALANCING: IT'S NOT NOTHING!

When talking about adopting a buy-and-hold strategy, it's important to remember that doing less than you think you should doesn't necessarily mean "set it and forget it." Investments get out of balance—meaning the asset allocation in your portfolio can change.

For instance, if you originally allocate 60 percent of your portfolio to stocks and the market experiences an increase, you may find that stocks now represent 80 percent of your portfolio. That means your portfolio is riskier than it was when you started, so it's a good idea to rebalance. In addition, it's a good idea to rebalance your portfolio when the conditions of the market change. For example, in a bear market (downward trending) you may want your portfolio to be more heavily weighted toward lower-risk bonds, whereas in a bull market (upward trending) you may want to shift toward stocks. There are three ways to rebalance your portfolio:

1. Sell some investments from overweighted asset categories and use the proceeds to make purchases in your underweighted asset categories.

2. Purchase new investments from the underweighted categories.

3. If you are still making regular and/or continuous contributions to your portfolio (as you are probably doing with your 401(k) or IRA), then you can change your contributions so that more of your investments are in the underweighted asset categories until your portfolio is rebalanced.

Regular rebalancing is an important part of keeping your portfolio healthy and in alignment with your investment goals. It is also something you should plan on doing no more frequently than every six to twelve months. More often than that, and you risk triggering the action bias.

Most workers who have invested in their company's retirement program will find that automatic annual rebalancing is part of the service offered through their 401(k). Check with your plan materials to determine if this is something you need to do manually, or if your retirement account already has rebalancing taken care of.

Long-Term Investing

It should be clear by now that investing rationally means taking the long view. But what if you don't have much time before you hope to retire? Are there different rules for investing when you have a shorter window?

While staring down the barrel of a retirement you don't feel prepared for is enough to make anyone desperate, it's important to remember that risky investments are a bad way of making up for having a low retirement account. As Dr. Crosby points out, get-rich-quick and get-poor-quick are two sides of the same coin. Suffice it to say, looking for investing to solve a short-term money problem is a good way to make your problem bigger. Take the long view with your investments, and your investments can take care of you.

Instead of looking for big returns, pre-retirees would do better to remember that retirement does not mean the end of investing. You can plan on keeping a portion of your portfolio in long-term, aggressive assets, so that you have time to ride out market volatility before you plan to use that money. This is part of an investment strategy known as the bucket method, and we will talk in detail about it in Chapter 5.

The main point here is to know what your tolerance for risk is—once you know something about the emotional state in which you approach investing, then you'll have a much better idea of how to invest with your head instead of your heart.

Chapter 3 Takeaways

1. Greed and fear drive the boom-and-bust cycles of the market. To be a rational investor, you must learn to be impervious to outside influence.

2. Risk is the absolute loss of capital, and it is highly personal and idiosyncratic.

3. Expert predictions are not reliable. Stick with statistical analysis rather than experts. Other than rebalancing your portfolio, do less than you think you should.

4. Investing should be used for long-term planning. There are no guaranteed quick bucks to be made.

CHAPTER 4

Figure Out What You Want from Retirement

WHAT YOU'LL LEARN IN THIS CHAPTER

In this chapter, you will explore what you value most as you plan for retirement, and you will set goals for creating the retirement of your dreams. In addition, you will also create a "Plan B" retirement that can offer you a contented life post-career in case your dream retirement is simply not in the cards. Finally, we will talk about how just as there is no such thing as Prince Charming, there is no Retirement Charming that will solve all of your problems.

Begin with the End in Mind

Stephen Covey, management expert and author of *The Seven Habits of Highly Effective People*, makes beginning with the end in mind the second habit you should adopt. Covey explains the importance of this habit by pointing out the fact that "all things are created twice. There's a mental or first creation, and a physical or second creation to all things."

This is the sort of advice that is obvious when you stop to think about it, but is very easily overlooked in the midst of a project. All too often, we are guilty of doing the same thing with our retirement planning—starting without the end in mind. If you start saving money for retirement without figuring out exactly what that retirement will look like, your life post-career may not be to your taste.

The solution to this very common problem is to take the time to figure exactly what you want from retirement.

Dream Big

Throughout our lives, we are often told both implicitly and explicitly that we need to lower our expectations for life. After all, it is important to be practical and recognize financial, logistical, and temperamental limitations to our biggest dreams.

However, dreaming big is the only way to really figure out what you want and value from your life. Once you have articulated your biggest retirement dreams, you can examine them to see what aspect of those dreams is so enticing to you. Take some time to do that now. Think about what your retirement would look like if money were no object, and write down your answers in Worksheet 4-1.

Worksheet 4-1: What Will the Retirement of My Dreams Look Like?

If the world were your oyster, how would you spend your time? Take a moment to think about how you would fill your days, weeks, months, and years in an ideal retirement. Actually jotting down your biggest retirement dreams will give you a goal to work toward, and it will also help you pinpoint what is most important to you.

1. Describe a typical day post-retirement.

You: ....

....

Your spouse: ....

....

2. Describe a typical week post-retirement.

You: ....

....

....

....

Your spouse: ....

....

....

....

3. Describe a typical month post-retirement.

You: ....

....

....

....

Your spouse: ....

....

....

....

4. Describe a typical year post-retirement.

You: ....

....

....

....

Your spouse: ....

....

....

....

Your dream retirement might be as grandiose as traveling the world in luxury, or it might be as simple as spending a lot of time with your grandchildren. But no matter what you dream of doing, there is an underlying value behind that big dream. Even if retirees cannot afford their exact vision of retirement, chances are they can fulfill the underlying value driving their dreams. For instance, retirees who want to spoil their grandchildren might value family and time spent with children. A cash-strapped Grandpa might not be able to see his far-flung grandchildren as often as he'd like, but he could Skype with them, create inventive letter-writing traditions, or even find ways to volunteer with local children in his community. He could live his values even without being able to afford his dream.

To pinpoint the underlying values of your dream retirement, you will use Worksheet 4-2: What Do You Value?, adapted from Tina Su's "Fifteen Questions to Discover Your Personal Mission" on her website Think Simple Now (*www.thinksimplenow.com*).

Worksheet 4-2: What Do You Value?

1. What activities/people/events/hobbies/projects make you smile?
You: ....
....
Your spouse: ....
....

2. What were your favorite things to do in the past? What about now?
You: ....
....
Your spouse: ....
....

3. What activities make you lose track of time?
You: ....
....
Your spouse: ....
....

4. What makes you feel good about yourself?

You: ....

....

Your spouse: ....

....

5. What would you regret not fully doing, being, or having in your life?

You: ....

....

Your spouse: ....

....

6. Based on the answers to the previous questions, quickly write down five words or phrases that represent your deepest values.

You: ....

....

Your spouse: ....

....

These questions may seem awfully loosey-goosey in a book about finances. However, answering them can help you to cut through the unnecessary goals you might be following because of societal expectations. Giving honest answers to the questions will help you determine your personal and specific path to a fulfilling retirement. Knowing what you value can help you figure out what you want to do in retirement, giving you a realistic goal.

Now that you have completed these questions about your values, let's go back to your dream retirement. Except this time, instead of imagining the world is your oyster, imagine that you don't have the money for your dream retirement. How could you evoke the same feeling without the money to back it?

Worksheet 4-3: What Do You Really Want from Your Dream?

1. What is the most expensive aspiration in your dream retirement?

You: ....

....

Your spouse: ....

....

Example: We dream of traveling all over the world in retirement.

2. If you were unable to fulfill that aspiration, what would be your biggest regret about not doing it?

You: ....

....

Your spouse: ....

....

Example: We would regret not being able to experience new places, new cultures, and new foods.

3. List some other activities that you could do to alleviate that regret.

You: ....

....

Your spouse: ....

....

Example: We could take ethnic cooking classes locally, take courses about the areas we're interested in, learn a new language, or host a foreign-exchange student.

Your Values-Driven Retirement

By now, it should be clear that while some aspirations you have may not be within financial reach, you can find a way to fulfill the basic *need* behind each of your aspirations if you are creative. This is what I call creating a values-driven retirement. Even more than a big-dream retirement, a retirement that is based on your values will be a fulfilling and contented experience.

In Worksheet 4-2 you came up with five values. I now want you to think about what your retirement will look like if you intentionally incorporate those values into your life. What will you do each day, week, month, and year, if you are trying to live according to your values?

Don't create this list quickly. Figuring out your values-driven retirement should be an intentional exercise that takes some time. You are trying to determine what you *actually* want rather than what you *think* you want. So take some time to turn over these questions in your mind before you put the answers down on paper. There is no hurry, and it can really help to sit with these issues for a little while to help you clear out external influences and get to the core of what you really want from your retirement.

Worksheet 4-4: What Will My Values-Driven Retirement Look Like?

Taking into account the things that are most important to me, this is how I will spend my time in retirement:

1. Describe a typical day post-retirement.

You: ....

....

Your spouse: ....

....

2. Describe a typical week post-retirement.

You: ....

....

Your spouse: ....

....

3. Describe a typical month post-retirement.

You:...

....

Your spouse:...

....

4. Describe a typical year post-retirement.

You:...

....

Your spouse:...

....

The benefit of creating a values-driven retirement is that it can come closer to your *ideal* retirement than your dream scenario could. Yes, it would be wonderful if we all had as much money as we needed to do whatever we wanted in retirement. However, even unlimited funds do not promise an ideal situation, because it does not guarantee that you are living according to your values. Creating a values-driven retirement plan means that you can find ways to live the life you want even if the money is not there for the specifics that you have dreamed about.

Creating a "Plan B" Retirement

In a perfect world, your values-driven retirement would be entirely within your financial grasp. If you have a good sense what you need to feel contented, I believe that the cost of that plan will not be overwhelming. However, situations and finances can change, and you might find yourself unable to afford your values-driven retirement, even if you have cut out all of the factors that are unnecessary.

This is why you need to come up with a "Plan B" retirement, just in case the money is not available.

WORST-CASE SCENARIO

The best way to go about creating your "Plan B" is to start with the worst-case scenario for your finances. You want to know the least amount of money on which you might find yourself living.

In order to calculate this, you will need to do two things: look up how much money you currently have saved, and determine how much your current savings plus Social Security and/or your pension will come to per month in income. Presuming you are unable to put away anything more, that monthly amount will be your worst-case scenario. (You can find an excellent retirement income calculator on the Vanguard website at *https://retirementplans.vanguard.com/VGApp/pe/pubeducation/calculators/RetirementIncomeCalc.jsf*.)

Learning just how little you might have to live on can be both horrifying and stimulating. It is scary to think about having to make do with very little money, and it can motivate you to focus on the importance of saving for retirement when you might otherwise be tempted to spend money.

Happy with Life

It is an excellent idea to think about the *least you need in order to feel satisfied* with your life. A retired friend of mine had very little money, but was perfectly satisfied living in a group home for low-income seniors. Not only did she have a safe place to live and three meals a day, but she loved having plenty of time to read and regular access to her local library. All in all, she had enough, even though her experience looked nothing like her dream retirement or even her values-driven retirement.

I would like you to once more think through what your retirement experience will be—but this time, I would like you to create a bare minimum "Plan B" retirement. What is the very least you will need to do/experience in retirement to feel fulfilled and content?

Worksheet 4-5: What Will My "Plan B" Retirement Look Like?

If I had to live on very little in retirement, this is what I would want my time to look like:

1. Describe a typical day post-retirement.

You: ....

....

Your spouse: ....

....

Example: I'd like to spend time reading each day and take walks with my spouse. Though neither of us like to cook, we can plan to make cooking something we do together each day to save money and make the chore more fun.

2. Describe a typical week post-retirement.

You: ....

....

Your spouse: ....

....

Example: We could reduce our expenses greatly by getting rid of our car, since we will not need it much. We would like to make sure we get to church every week and visit the library at least once a week, and we know that we could easily get rides from family and friends for those weekly trips. For grocery shopping and the like, we can take the bus.

3. Describe a typical month post-retirement.

You: ....

....

Your spouse: ....

....

Example: Ideally, we would love to dine out once a week, but we can plan to make it a monthly or bimonthly splurge instead. I'd also like to spend time with family at least once a month in addition to seeing them every week at church.

4. Describe a typical year post-retirement.

You: ....

....

Your spouse: ....

....

Example: We know that taking a yearly vacation is not in the cards, but we would still like to plan some sort of annual treat, like an inexpensive local bus tour or camping within a couple of hours of our home. The cost of joining a bus tour or renting a car will be much lower than a vacation we have to fly to, or the cost of maintaining a car year-round.

Now that you have thought through your big dreams, your most important values, and the least you need, you are ready to plan for retirement. You can begin with three potential endings in mind—and with each ending, you have the possibility of enjoying a retirement that is specifically tailored to your taste.

BEWARE RETIREMENT CHARMING

In their groundbreaking book *Your Money or Your Life*, Vicki Robin and Joe Dominguez describe a scenario that we have all experienced—searching for what they call Job Charming: "It's as though we believed that there is a Job Charming out there—like the Prince Charming in fairy tales—that will fill our needs and inspire us to greatness. We've come to believe that, through this job, we would somehow have it all: status, meaning, adventure, travel, luxury, respect, power, tough challenges, and fantastic rewards."

For many of us, even if we have come to realize that our jobs will never fulfill us completely—that they will never be Job Charming—we still pin our hopes on Retirement Charming. *Once I retire, I'll be happy* is how this thinking goes.

But just as no one person and no one job can solve all of your problems and make you happy, no retirement is going to do that either. Looking for your retirement to give you the fulfillment you've been missing throughout your life is a good way to be disappointed in retirement.

My friend who was content to live in a group home in reduced circumstance was a contented person through much of her life. Her circumstances changed, but her outlook did not.

This is why it is so important to take the time to figure out the specific things that you value, that make your life meaningful, and that make you feel satisfied. Without them, it does not matter how much or how little money you have in the bank.

Chapter 4 Takeaways

1. Know where you want to end up in retirement, or you might find you are living a life that is not to your taste.

2. Dream big about retirement. It will help you determine what you truly value.

3. Creating a values-driven retirement should not be overwhelmingly expensive.

4. Knowing what your bare minimums are for the retired life can help you to protect the aspects of retirement that are most important to you.

5. Retiring will not solve your problems, but choosing the right retirement path will help make you more satisfied with life.

PART II

Debunking Retirement Myths

There's an awful lot of information about retirement out there, thanks in good part to the Internet. Sadly, a lot of it is wrong. In this section, we'll examine some of the common misconceptions about retirement and how you can replace mistaken ideas with clear, workable strategies to achieve the retirement lifestyle you want.

CHAPTER 5

Retirement Income Myths

WHAT YOU'LL LEARN IN THIS CHAPTER

In this chapter, we'll discuss why it's important to create your own retirement income goals rather than rely on what "everybody does." You will learn how to calculate an appropriate and personal metric for determining the right size nest egg for you. And you will learn the best way to withdraw money each year without having to worry about outliving your money.

Like any complicated system and difficult-to-understand subject, planning for retirement tends to attract its share of plausible-sounding myths. For instance, you've probably heard things like:

- *You need $1 million to retire comfortably.*
- *You need to replace 80 percent of your final salary in retirement.*
- *You can safely withdraw 4 percent from your nest egg each year in retirement and still maintain the principal.*

I have a love-hate relationship with these sorts of myths. On the one hand, even repeating misconceptions as fact at least gets people thinking and talking about retirement, which we need to do more of.

However, the sorts of general rules that become enshrined as myth all have the same problem: They ignore the highly individual nature of income, budgeting, retirement planning, and psychology. Following these myths can derail the very goals you're trying to achieve.

Let's start by considering some of the most common retirement myths:

Myth #1: You Need $1 Million to Retire Comfortably

This pervasive idea has a lot going for it: $1 million is a nice, round number to aim for, and for the majority of us, it's almost inconceivable that a cool million wouldn't be enough to live on for twenty-five to thirty years.

Unfortunately, this myth is inaccurate to the point of being counterproductive.

To start, $1 million isn't the huge sum it once was (as Dr. Evil of the Austin Powers movies found out, much to his chagrin). Depending on the particular retirement path you choose to follow, you might find that a million-dollar nest egg is nowhere near enough for the retirement of your dreams. This is a big part of the reason why in Chapter 4 you figured out exactly what you want from retirement. Unless you have calculated how much your retirement plan will cost, just assuming that $1 million will cover it is naive. The fact of the matter is that, depending on your cost of living and circumstances, it's possible to exhaust a million-dollar nest egg with typical and relatively modest retirement spending.

On the other side of the coin, even though $1 million could be considered a modest nest egg for many retirement plans, it's still a number that can be out of reach for the majority of workers. According to a study reported in the *Wall Street Journal* by market research firm Phoenix, in 2013 there were about 6.15 million American households worth $1 million or more, not including the value of real estate. That translates to 5 percent, or one in every twenty households. For many of the other nineteen households, the idea of saving $1 million for retirement can sound as overwhelming as planning to retire to the moon. That intimidation factor can be enough to make some people give up on saving altogether.

A NEST EGG EQUAL TO EIGHT
TIMES YOUR FINAL SALARY

In order for a rule of thumb to be effective, it must take at least some of your personal metrics into account. Saving an amount equal to eight times your final salary—this suggestion was created and espoused by Fidelity—is useful because it is based on your personal income rather than an arbitrary dollar amount.

This rule of thumb assumes that you will need to replace about 85 percent of your final income in retirement (which we will discuss in depth later in this chapter), although it allows for some wiggle room depending on when you began saving, when you plan to retire, how much you save per year, your annual salary growth, your salary replacement needs in retirement, your life expectancy, and your expected rate of return. Based upon those seven variables, Fidelity calculates that you can retire comfortably if you have about eight times your final salary in the bank at retirement.

Fidelity further breaks down this rule into suggestions of the amount of salary you'll need to save: one year's worth by age thirty-five, three years' salary by age forty-five, and five years' salary by age fifty-five. Using this metric, you can figure out if you are on track. You can do your own calculations based upon this rule of thumb at *https://www.fidelity.com/ viewpoints/retirement/8X-retirement-savings*.

Myth #2: Replace 80 Percent of Your Final Salary in Retirement

While this myth is not as arbitrary as the $1 million rule, it still does not take into account nearly enough of your personal circumstances. That's because how much you need to retire on depends entirely on your intended retirement activities. If you plan to travel the world, you'll need far more income than if you want to become the world's foremost expert on daytime television. In addition, if your health deteriorates, you'll need more retirement income than you would if you stay healthy as a horse in your golden years. It makes more sense to calculate your actual expenses in retirement rather than assume that living on 80 percent of your pre-retirement income will cut it.

Both the $1 million nest-egg myth and this myth don't take into account the most important aspect of your retirement income: how you plan to spend it. One million is an arbitrary number, and focusing on your pre-retirement income is irrelevant when compared to your expenses.

ABOUT TWENTY-FIVE TIMES YOUR ANNUAL RETIREMENT EXPENSES

The best way to determine how large a nest egg you will need is to specifically calculate your basic annual retirement expenses. From there, you will estimate your anticipated investment returns, giving you an idea of how much you need in total to retire comfortably.

Start this with Worksheet 5-1:

WORKSHEET 5-1
Calculating Basic Retirement Expenses

CATEGORY	COST
Rent/mortgage:	
Car payment:	
Groceries and household items:	
Dining out:	
Gasoline:	
Public transportation:	
Electric bill:	
Gas bill:	
Water bill:	
Trash pickup bill:	
Cable/Internet/satellite bill:	
Telephone bill:	

Cell phone bill:
....

Credit card/loan payments:
....

Personal care (haircuts, etc.):
....

Health/dental insurance:
....

Subscriptions:
....

Memberships:
....

Property taxes:
....

Homeowners insurance:
....

Car insurance:
....

Miscellaneous:
....

TOTAL:

Now multiply that number by twelve in order to determine your yearly retirement expenses:

$$\text{.......................} \times 12 = \text{.......................}$$

These calculations are for a basic retirement. We will talk more about specific retirement expenses for various types of retirement in the final part of the book.

Now that you have an idea of your annual retirement expenses (which may or may not be anywhere near 80 percent of your pre-retirement income), it's time to use that figure to calculate a sufficient nest egg. To do this, you will need to estimate your investment returns—accounting for inflation, which averages around 3 percent per year. (That means if you think you will see 7 percent returns overall, you will calculate it as 4 percent.) You will divide your estimated rate (as a decimal) into one in order to find your multiplier—that is, the amount you have to multiply your annual expenses by in order to determine your nest-egg needs. You can see how this is done in Table 5-2.

TABLE 5-2:
Determining Your Expenses Multiplier

RETURN RATE (ACCOUNTING FOR INFLATION)	DIVIDED INTO 1	MULTIPLIER
3%	1/0.03 = 33.33	33 × Your Annual Expenses
4%	1/0.04 = 25	25 × Your Annual Expenses
5%	1/0.05 = 20	20 × Your Annual Expenses

Since 4 percent real returns (after factoring in inflation) is a conservative assumption for your investments, most people can safely assume that twenty-five times their annual retirement expenses will be a sufficient nest egg. Under this assumption, you would plan to withdraw 4 percent from your nest egg per year while protecting the principal—although we will talk more about this assumption in the next section.

The number that you come up with by using these calculations could be much larger or smaller than $1 million, and annual expenses may be nowhere near 80 percent of your income. The important thing is that the expense and nest-egg amounts you came up with are based upon your specific circumstances—which means you can tweak those circumstances in order to make an overwhelming number more manageable or a modest number more aspirational.

Myth #3: Withdrawing 4 Percent per Year Will Maintain Your Principal

The 4 percent withdrawal rule, which is also known as systematic withdrawal, is one of the most common methods for figuring retirement income. It's a simple system, which helps to explain its popularity. The idea behind this system is that you can safely withdraw 4 percent of your assets each year in retirement without touching the principal. This myth assumes that your investments will grow by at least 4 percent each year, so no withdrawal will cut into your principal. For instance, a retiree with a $1 million nest egg could withdraw $40,000 each year without worrying about the principal.

IF THE MARKET IS DOWN

Unfortunately, as anyone who planned to retire in 2008 can tell you, the 4 percent withdrawal rule has some serious drawbacks. If you need to make a withdrawal while the market is experiencing a big downturn, as it did in 2008–09, you will find yourself in the unenviable position of either living on less that year, or taking the 4 percent you'd planned on taking and diminishing your principal. If the market is down at the beginning of your retirement, then you may find that your temporary losses become permanent.

As it turns out, the idea that you can safely withdraw 4 percent per year without doing any other strategic asset allocation is a myth. Between 1994, when financial adviser William Bengen proposed this withdrawal strategy, and the 2008–2009 market correction was a kind of mythical "golden age," and that timing was the only reason why it seemed possible to count on the 4 percent withdrawal strategy.

USE THE BUCKET METHOD

The big problem with the 4 percent method is that it assumes that "average" is the same as "always." For instance, from 2004 to 2013 the market averaged a return of 7.34 percent, according to calculations made by the New York University Stern School of Business based on raw data from the Federal Reserve. If your investments *always* had a return of 7.34 percent, there would be no problems with the 4 percent withdrawal rule—and in fact it might seem a little conservative. However, in 2008, the average return marketwide was an alarming –36.55 percent. Having returns for a single year that are not only low but that eat into your principal could completely destroy your retirement plan. This casts the wisdom of the 4 percent rule in a much different light.

Instead of using your nest egg as a single return-generating entity, it's better to place your money into various buckets that will work for you at different times in retirement. That way, you start with the assumption that you will have to ride out some market volatility during your golden years—and you plan ahead for it.

In order to do this, you will split your portfolio into separate income "buckets," each of which will be intended to handle a different time period in retirement.

The most common way to allocate buckets is to separate them into three asset classes and time periods:

1. **Years 1–5.** Your first bucket is intended to take care of your finances in the first five years of retirement. Since you want both stability and liquidity in this time period, the money in this bucket will be placed in cash-equivalent assets, where you know that the principal is protected. Cash equivalents include CDs, U.S. Treasury bills, and money market funds. Having the money in this bucket will provide you with the stability you need to know that your principal (and income) for the first five years of your retirement will be protected, while still giving the remainder of your money in the other two buckets the time it needs to continue to grow.

2. **Years 6–15.** The second bucket will take care of your retirement income during the middle portion of your retirement—about year six through year fifteen. Since you will not be tapping this money until you have gotten a few years into your retirement, you can afford to be a little more aggressive with your investments. For most retirees, the second bucket will consist of more of a mix of bonds and stocks, leaning more toward the safety of bonds. While you do have the time to ride out market fluctuations with this bucket, you still want to ensure that your money will be there once you reach this time period. Allocating your assets in such a way that will reasonably protect the principal while providing the opportunity to grow is the goal of this bucket.

3. Years 16 and further. The third bucket is where you should be most aggressive in your investments, because you will not be accessing the money in this portion of your portfolio until after you have been retired for about fifteen years. With this money you can afford to invest in high-risk/high-return assets, such as stocks and other types of equities. With the additional time on your side, you can both ride out the volatility of the market and reap the potential benefits.

As the years go by, you'll need to rebalance your assets from one bucket to another in order to continue to meet each portion's goals. For instance, as you use up the funds in your first bucket, you will need to move some of the second bucket's funds into the first bucket and move some of the third bucket's funds into the second. While these redistributions may not always be necessary—for instance, if the market is doing well and your returns are such that each bucket has maintained or exceeded your goals—you will have to keep a regular eye on how your three-part portfolio is doing.

Since each bucket will have certain goals tied to it, the strategy can help to ensure retirees remain disciplined in their withdrawals and their spending. In addition, breaking the overwhelming task of allocating assets for retirement into three smaller goals can relieve a great deal of stress.

Using this retirement withdrawal strategy can potentially help make retirement possible for those who have not saved as much as they might like. Since you are investing a portion of your money for the long term, you could theoretically end your career before you've reached your ideal nest-egg amount—something you cannot do if you plan to use the 4 percent withdrawal rule. The bucket method allows for a great deal more flexibility than the 4 percent rule, so it can work better for everyone, whether you are forced to retire early or you got a late start in saving. (Just remember that there are no guarantees—so even if you are willing to let compound interest do its magic on your third bucket of investments, always hedge your bets.)

Chapter 5 Takeaways

1. One million is an arbitrary amount of money. It will be out of reach for some and far too little for others.

2. Basing your retirement nest-egg needs on your pre-retirement income ignores how you will actually use your retirement income—for expenses.

3. Most workers will find that saving either twenty-five times their calculated annual retirement expenses or eight times their final salary will provide them with a sufficient nest egg.

4. A 4 percent retirement withdrawal can only keep your principal safe in good times. When the market is down, your principal is vulnerable under this strategy.

5. Allocating your portfolio into at least three time-based "buckets" is the best way to protect your principal and allow for a flexible retirement.

CHAPTER 6

Social Security Myths

WHAT YOU'LL LEARN IN THIS CHAPTER

By the end of this chapter, you will understand how your Social Security benefits will fit into your retirement income. You will learn exactly how the Social Security program works, and be able to separate the facts from the myths about the program's health and projected longevity. You will understand the relationship between your income, the FICA taxes you pay during your career, and the benefits you are eligible for in retirement. You will learn how taxes will affect your benefit checks, and you will understand why taking benefits as early as possible is not the ideal way to retire.

You can't watch a news segment on retirement without hearing a pundit, politician, or tax professional warning the viewers about the uncertain future of our Social Security system. These concerns can seem especially terrifying considering the fact that Social Security benefits are the major source of income for most of the elderly—representing at least half of the retirement income for 74 percent of single beneficiaries and 52 percent of married couples.

Since Social Security is an important part of American finances, worries about how long the Social Security Trust Fund will last and where the money goes are inevitable. With so many people relying on their Social Security benefits as a major source of income, Americans can't help but be concerned about the money drying up. It's understandable that we often react emotionally to negative projections about the program. However, as we have learned in previous chapters, negative projections and downturns do not have to spell disaster, whether we are talking about your investment portfolio or the Social Security Trust Fund.

Social Security Myth #1: Social Security Is about to Go Bankrupt

The Social Security Administration is an enormous government entity. As such, it has all of the complexity inherent in any program that services over 59 million Americans. That complexity makes it very difficult for any individual news segment or article to adequately explain the specifics of Social Security finances, which means most media treatments of the program rely on shortcuts to make their point.

In particular, you will often hear that Social Security payments exceed payroll tax revenues—which is absolutely true. Between 1985 and 2009, the taxes coming in to pay for Social Security exceeded the expenses for the program. The surplus that came in during those years (and in every year that income exceeded expenses) was placed in the Social Security Trust Fund where it earned interest. Starting in 2010, the yearly expenses for the program exceeded the tax revenue brought in, and that is expected to be the case for the foreseeable future. According to the Social Security Administration, the Social Security Trust Fund began losing value as of 2013, and will become entirely depleted in 2037.

As frightening as these facts may be, they only tell a portion of the story. Just because Social Security's expenses currently exceed tax revenues doesn't mean that the sky is falling or even that Social Security is well on its way to becoming nothing more than an ID-generator. That's because this myth ignores the reality of how Social Security works.

IT IS IMPOSSIBLE FOR SOCIAL SECURITY TO GO BANKRUPT

We tend to think of Social Security as solely a retirement program, despite the fact that over a quarter of benefits are paid to disabled workers, survivors of deceased workers, and the dependents of both groups. Because of that mental association with retirement, there is a common misconception that Social Security works something like a pension fund, into which you put money when you are young and from which you draw money when you retire.

However, that is not now, nor has it ever been, how the program works. Social Security works as an immediate transfer from current workers to current beneficiaries. That means it's not possible for the program to "run out of money" because the program is not counting on a specific pool of money. Instead, it counts on the tax revenue of current workers. Unlike a pension fund, the tax revenue we count on for benefits can't become insolvent.

THE SOCIAL SECURITY TRUST FUND'S THREE REVENUE STREAMS

The fact that Social Security can't go "bankrupt" may sound like semantics when you remember that Social Security benefits exceed the tax revenue that pays for them. However, it's important to remember that Social Security has planned ahead for this situation by making sure the program has two additional income streams to supplement the payroll taxes that pay for immediate benefits.

During years that taxes exceeded benefits, the surplus was placed in the Social Security Trust Fund, where it earns interest. That interest, along with the income tax paid on Social Security benefits by beneficiaries with high incomes, are the two additional revenue streams for the program. (We will talk in detail about income tax on benefits later in this chapter.) When you include all three revenue sources in your calculations, you will find that the Social Security Administration is actually running a surplus (which was over $32 billion in 2013), and that those surpluses are slated to continue until the year 2020.

However, even when you count all three income streams, without action from Congress, the Trust Fund will be depleted in a couple of decades. At that time, each year's tax revenue is projected to pay for 75 percent of the benefits currently promised. This is the shortfall that many pundits are referring to when they describe the possibility of "bankruptcy."

WHAT ABOUT THE WORKER-TO-RETIREE RATIO?

The system set in place where current workers pay for current benefits works pretty well when the ratio of workers and retirees is well balanced. But what happens when a huge number of workers retire all at the same time?

The 76 million baby boomers who began reaching age sixty-two (the earliest age you can collect retirement benefits) as of 2008 could theoretically place an enormous burden on our Social Security system. Between the size of the generation (the largest in American history) and their increased life expectancy compared to their parents and grandparents, it may seem as though we as a country cannot afford for boomers to retire.

However, seeing this generation retire is hardly a sudden shock. As Virginia P. Reno and Joni Lavery point out in their Social Security Brief *Can We Afford Social Security When Baby Boomers Retire?*, "While baby boomers may have been a surprise when they turned up in record numbers to enroll in kindergarten in the 1950s, their retirement six decades later is not. Policymakers began to plan as early as 1983, when Congress lowered the cost of Social Security benefits for boomers and later generations by raising the age at which unreduced retirement benefits will be paid." By making tweaks to benefit amounts and full retirement age over time, Social Security has helped to prepare for the next phase of the boomers' lives. The projected Social Security shortfall could be more than taken care of with a slight increase to Social Security payroll taxes, a slight reduction in benefits, and/or a slight increase in full retirement age. Considering the popularity of the program, it is likely that our politicians will make some or all of those changes before we reach that shortfall.

Social Security Myth #2: Your Benefits Are Based on Your Last Ten Years of Employment

This common misconception probably stems from the fact that workers need about ten years of payment into payroll taxes in order to collect retirement benefits. But that minimum work history is not related to the way that Social Security calculates your benefits. The calculation is somewhat complicated—your payments are based on your thirty-five highest-earning years (adjusted for inflation)—but the complex calculations allow for the fairest possible distribution of benefits.

Rather than make retirement decisions based on misconceptions about your role as a taxpayer and a beneficiary, it is much better to understand the complexities of Social Security's calculations so you can determine what is best for you.

HOW SOCIAL SECURITY WORKS FOR TAXPAYERS

Regularly employed individuals will see 6.2 percent of their gross earnings taxed for Social Security. In addition, your employer also kicks in 6.2 percent, making the total tax contribution 12.4 percent of your gross income. However, there is an income limit on Social Security taxation, which as of 2015 is $118,500. Any income you earn above that limit is not taxed. That means that you will not have to pay more than $7,347.00 (6.2 percent of $118,500) in Social Security taxes in 2015— although the income limit goes up every year.

If you are self-employed, you are considered to be both employer and employee, which means you have to pay the full 12.4 percent of Social Security taxes yourself.

Working and paying taxes toward Social Security earns you "credits" through the Social Security program. As of 2015, a taxpayer earns one credit for every $1,220 he or she earns at work, up to a maximum of four credits per year. The credit amount is generally readjusted each year. You will need forty total credits (that is, ten years of work) in order to qualify for retirement benefits.

HOW SOCIAL SECURITY WORKS
FOR BENEFICIARIES

Your Social Security benefits are based upon two things: your earnings history and your age at enrollment.

Your benefits are calculated using the thirty-five highest-earning years in your career. That's great news for a sixty-five-year-old retiree who has been working steadily since he was seventeen years old. With forty-eight years of work history to choose from, Social Security will be able to calculate his benefits based on the thirty-five years he made the most money.

If, however, you have less than thirty-five years of work experience, the Social Security Administration uses zeros to create the average for the calculation, lowering your average earnings and your payout. If you don't have thirty-five years of employment history, it's a good idea to continue working to get those zeros replaced in your Social Security calculation.

As for your age, Social Security changes the benefit amount based on whether you retire before or after your full retirement age. Basically, the longer you wait, the more money you will see in your benefit checks.

This is why it is generally not advisable for you to take Social Security benefits at age sixty-two, even though you are eligible for them at that time. If you take early benefits, your payments will be *permanently reduced*. In order to collect your full benefit, you will need to wait until you have reached your full retirement age, which depends upon your birth year.

The closer you are to your full retirement age when you take benefits, the smaller your benefit reduction will be. In addition, if you delay taking benefits past your full retirement age, then your monthly payments will increase by 8 percent every year that you delay until you reach age seventy. So until you reach your seventieth birthday, the longer you wait to claim your benefits, the more money you will see in each monthly payment.

To find out what your specific monthly benefit will be, the Social Security Administration uses a complex formula to first index your earnings (that is, to adjust your earnings to account for average wage changes over the years), and then calculate your benefits.

Good Things Come to Those Who Wait

As of 2012, 37.2 percent of new Social Security retirement benefits for men and 42.4 percent of new benefits for women were awarded to sixty-two-year-olds. While collecting benefits as soon as you are eligible is not necessarily the wrong decision for your specific circumstances, it is difficult to believe that it is the right financial decision for the number of beneficiaries who elect to do so. Deferring your benefits for even one year can make a big difference in your retirement income—and waiting until you reach your full retirement age (and full benefits) can often outweigh the years of benefits checks you missed by waiting. You'd hate to kick yourself for being impatient.

Thankfully, at least the customer service side of the Social Security Administration has embraced the twenty-first century, and there are a number of very user-friendly calculators and applications on their website to help you figure out your potential benefits without forcing you to sharpen any pencils or start counting on your fingers and toes. In particular, you can use the benefits calculators at *www.socialsecurity.gov/planners/benefitcalculators.html* to enter your information and learn what you can expect from your benefits. In addition, signing up for a *"my* Social Security" account at *www.socialsecurity.gov/myaccount/* can provide both workers and retirees with a great deal of information about your Social Security earnings record and benefits.

Social Security Myth #3: Your Social Security Benefits Are Not Taxed

There is an excellent reason why you might believe this particular myth: According to the Social Security Administration, only about 40 percent of beneficiaries pay federal taxes on their benefits. For the majority of beneficiaries, there is no need to worry that Uncle Sam will take his cut of your benefit checks.

However, there is a flip side to this myth. Many people alternatively believe that their Social Security benefits are fully taxed. For most of the people who believe this, getting that first untaxed benefit check must be a pleasant surprise.

It is understandable why two completely opposing myths about taxes on Social Security benefits are both widely believed: The rules for taxing benefits are extremely complicated. It's much easier to wrap your head around an all-or-nothing taxation. However, you should know what to expect when it comes to taxes on your benefits so that you can adequately plan.

DETERMINING THE TAXES ON YOUR SOCIAL SECURITY BENEFITS

Unless your retirement income is less than a certain amount, you can expect to pay taxes on anywhere from 50 percent to 85 percent of a portion your Social Security benefits.

The calculation for determining if your benefits are taxable is deceptively simple. In order to figure out if you owe Uncle Sam any money, you will add together:

1. One-half of your Social Security benefits, plus

2. All your other income, including tax-exempt interest. (While tax-exempt interest is included in this calculation, tax-free distributions from your Roth IRA are not.)

The amount that you come up with is then compared to the following base amounts in order to determine how much of your Social Security benefits are taxed (if any).

TABLE 6-1:

Base Amounts to Determine Taxable Social Security

If You File As	Then Your Base Amount Is	And You Will Owe Taxes on This Percentage of Your Social Security Benefits	Your Additional Amount Is	And You Will Owe Taxes on This Percentage of Your Social Security Benefits
Single	$25,000	50%	$34,000	85%
Married, Filing Jointly	$32,000	50%	$44,000	85%

If your income falls below the lower base amount, then you will owe no taxes on your Social Security benefits. If your income falls between the lower and upper base amounts, you will owe taxes on up to 50 percent of your benefits. And if your income is greater than the upper base amount, then you will owe taxes on no more than 85 percent of your benefits.

As if these calculations weren't confusing enough, knowing the amount of benefits that are taxable does not actually indicate how much money you are going to owe the IRS come tax time. The taxable amount of your benefits just gives you the number of dollars you will owe taxes on—not how much is taken from your benefits to pay those taxes. Those benefits are taxed at your marginal tax rate, which is determined based upon your level of income. Use the following chart to determine your marginal tax rate:

TABLE 6-2:

2015 Marginal Tax Rates

MARGINAL TAX RATE	SINGLE FILER INCOME	MARRIED, FILING JOINTLY INCOME
10%	up to $9,225	up to $18,450
15%	$9,225 to $37,450	$18,450 to $74,900
25%	$37,450 to $90,750	$74,900 to $151,200
28%	$90,750 to $189,300	$151,200 to $230,450
33%	$189,300 to $411,500	$230,450 to $411,500
35%	$411,500 to $413,200	$411,500 to $464,850
39.6%	$413,200+	$464,850+

Remember, the marginal tax rate is only the rate you pay on the highest portion of your income. Which is to say, if you fall in the 25 percent tax bracket, you are not taxed 25 percent on all of your income. You are taxed 25 percent on any income above $37,450 (if you are single), you are taxed 15 percent on any income between $9,225 and $37,450, and you are taxed 10 percent on any income below $9,225.

Now that you know how to calculate what portion of your Social Security benefits will be taxed, take the time to estimate what that portion will be with Worksheet 6-3. Use the benefit calculator at *www.socialsecurity.gov/planners/benefitcalculators.html* to come up with projected Social Security benefits, and take the time to estimate your projected retirement income based upon your savings. With these two figures, you can fill out this worksheet:

Worksheet 6-3: IRS Worksheet 1—Figuring Your Taxable Benefits

1. Enter your total Social Security benefits ....

2. Enter one-half of line 1 ....

3. Enter your other taxable income ....

4. Add lines 2 and 3 ....

5. Enter the base amount for your filing status ($25,000 for single filers, $32,000 for married taxpayers filing jointly) ....

6. Subtract line 5 from line 4. If zero or less, enter -0- ....

7. Enter $9,000 if single, or $12,000 if married filing jointly. (This number is the difference between the base amount and the additional amount. That is, it's the difference between $25,000 and $34,000 for single filers and the difference between $32,000 and $44,000 for taxpayers who are married, filing jointly) ....

8. Subtract line 7 from line 6. If zero or less, enter -0- ....

9. Enter the smaller of line 6 or line 7. ....

10. Enter one-half of line 9. ....

11. Enter the smaller of line 2 or line 10. ....

12. Multiply line 8 by 85% (0.85). If line 8 is zero, enter -0- ....

13. Add lines 11 and 12 ....

14. Multiply line 1 by 85% (0.85) ....

15. Taxable Benefits. Enter the smaller of line 13 or line 14. ....

Chapter 6 Takeaways

1. Social Security benefits are funded by current tax revenues, which means it is impossible for Social Security to go "bankrupt." However, there is a projected shortfall between promised benefits and future tax revenues starting in about two decades.

2. Accounting for all three of Social Security's revenue streams (tax revenues, Trust Fund interest, and taxes on benefits), the program will run a surplus until 2020.

3. Benefits are calculated based upon your thirty-five highest-earning years (adjusted for inflation).

4. Taking benefits prior to reaching full retirement age means your benefits will be permanently reduced.

5. You may pay taxes on no more than 85 percent of your Social Security benefits if you enjoy a high income in retirement.

CHAPTER 7

Medicare and Healthcare Myths

WHAT YOU'LL LEARN IN THIS CHAPTER

In this chapter, we will discuss the potentially enormous impact of healthcare and medical costs on your retirement. First, you will learn just how expensive healthcare in retirement can be, and we will discuss several strategies for ensuring that a health problem in retirement doesn't completely derail your finances. You will understand the specifics of what Medicare covers and how much it will cost. And you will learn what additional insurance you should consider in order to protect your health and your finances.

When it comes to healthcare in retirement, people tend to believe two very detrimental myths:

1. An expensive health problem isn't going to happen to *me*.

2. If I do get sick, Medicare will take care of me.

The first myth is rooted in human nature. We tend to ignore the likelihood of something bad happening to us because we think bad things happen to other people. Our minds have difficulty grasping that we're vulnerable to unexpected disasters, so we respond by disbelieving in their possibility.

The second myth stems from lack of information. Americans tend to believe that Medicare is the end-all and be-all of health insurance for retirees. But the Medicare program covers less than you might think, and the program costs beneficiaries more out-of-pocket than you might expect. Entering into retirement without a good understanding of how you will handle your healthcare costs and Medicare needs is a recipe for disaster.

Healthcare Is Going to Cost More Than You Think

Each year, Fidelity Benefits Consulting calculates the average cost of medical expenses for a sixty-five-year-old couple retiring during that calendar year. In 2014, Fidelity calculated that the average couple will need $220,000 in today's dollars to cover their medical expenses throughout retirement.

What's even more alarming than the astronomical dollar figure is the fact that Fidelity based its calculations on sixty-five-year-old retirees—meaning the hypothetical retiring couple is already eligible for Medicare. In addition, that price tag does not include the cost of nursing-home care (which is not covered by Medicare).

The sad fact is that healthcare is likely to be one of your biggest expenses in retirement, and it's one that often takes retirees by surprise. According to Ashlea Ebeling of Forbes.com, a recent poll of pre-retirees ranging in age from fifty-five to sixty-four found that 48 percent of those polled believed that they would only need about $50,000 set aside for healthcare costs in retirement.

Workers tend to underestimate their retirement healthcare costs because very few of them take the time to calculate their specific healthcare needs. If you go into retirement with only a vague idea of how much medical care will cost and what particular medical issues you might be facing, there is no way you can be fully prepared for the actual costs of healthcare in retirement.

Obviously, thinking about what kinds of ailments you might suffer in your old age and how much it will cost to alleviate those ailments is up there with unmedicated dental work in sheer entertainment value.

However, as unpleasant as it might be to think about whether your grandfather's lumbago and gout are hereditary, it is much worse to have medical needs and no money to pay for them. That's why you should take the time to calculate your specific retirement healthcare needs.

The AARP Health Expense Calculator

AARP offers an excellent tool for calculating the cost of healthcare in retirement. The calculator allows you to plug in your current age, projected retirement age, projected life expectancy, height and weight, health habits, and the specific diseases or health concerns you expect to suffer from. Based upon the information you provide, the calculator offers you an estimate of your total healthcare costs in retirement, broken down into the amount covered by Medicare and the amount you will be responsible for out of pocket. In addition, the calculator offers further reading on how to improve your health through lifestyle changes. You can find the link to this calculator at *www.aarp.org/work/work_tools/*.

SAVING FOR YOUR HEALTHCARE NEEDS

Once you recognize the need to save money specifically for your healthcare in retirement, you have options that can help you prepare financially—and minimize your tax burden, to boot. Specifically, you can either start saving money in a Health Savings Account or in a Roth IRA.

Health Savings Accounts

Health Savings Accounts (HSAs) are similar to traditional IRAs in that contributions up to the legal limit are 100 percent tax-deductible, and the money in the HSA grows tax-deferred. In addition, withdrawals you make in order to pay for qualified medical expenses are not taxed at all—not even earned interest, as long as it is used for medical expenses. Unlike Flexible Spending Accounts, you do not have to use the money in your HSA within a year or risk forfeiting it. The money in your HSA is yours to keep.

In addition, while you cannot make non-medical withdrawals from an HSA prior to age sixty-five without incurring a 20 percent tax penalty and income tax, any non-medical withdrawals made after age sixty-five are penalty-free (but still subject to income tax).

As long as you use your HSA funds for qualified medical expenses—which include deductibles, copayment, coinsurance, and any care that is not covered by your health insurance—then your money is entirely tax-free. You fund the HSA with pre-tax dollars, pay no taxes on HSA fund growth, and pay no taxes when you withdraw funds for your medical expenses.

Like IRAs, HSAs have contribution limits with catch-up provisions for individuals who are fifty-five or older. Table 7-1 outlines the limits for 2015:

TABLE 7-1:
HSA Contribution Limits in 2015

	CONTRIBUTION LIMIT	55+ CATCH-UP CONTRIBUTION
Single	$3,350	$1,000
Family	$6,650	$1,000

Before you start asking where to sign up, it is important to remember that there are some relatively major drawbacks to Health Savings Accounts. As good a savings vehicle as they are, HSAs are not for everyone, and for good reason.

Health Savings Account Drawbacks
Having an HSA is not as simple as just putting money aside for future health concerns. Eligibility for a Health Savings Account requires you to be signed up for a high-deductible health plan (HDHP) with no other health insurance coverage. (This restriction on other health insurance coverage does not include disability and long-term care insurance.)

In 2015, the minimum deductible for an HDHP to qualify for a Health Savings Account is $1,300 for an individual and $2,600 for a family. (Remember, these are the *minimums* required by the government for an HDHP to be eligible for a Health Savings Account. You may find plans with higher deductibles.)

When you are insured with an HDHP policy, you must meet the entire deductible for the year before the insurance will pony up any payments. While some high-deductible plans will pay for 100 percent of your covered expenses once the deductible is met, most do not. In 2015, the government has set the maximum out-of-pocket expenses for an HDHP for a single participant at $6,450 and at $12,900 for a family. So an individual insured with an HDHP will have to pay all expenses out of pocket until she reaches the deductible of $1,300, and then she will pay a percentage of any remaining medical expenses until hitting the $6,450 cap, at which point the insurer will pay all further expenses.

If you decide to save money for your healthcare expenses in retirement with an HSA, then you will be facing potentially hefty costs:

- Premiums for the HDHP (which, to be fair, are low)
- The deductible
- Uncovered medical expenses
- Any copayments or coinsurance required by your plan once you have met the deductible until you reach the spending cap
- HSA contributions for your medical costs in retirement

Saving money for your retirement healthcare expenses with an HSA can clearly be a bit of a gamble, particularly if you are in less-than-perfect health. Any health hiccups, and you might find that you are using the HSA you put in place to save for the future to pay for your medical care right now. It's a classic Catch-22: If you are in such excellent health that you know your HSA savings will actually be in place when you need it in the future, you're less likely to need a huge healthcare nest egg in the first place.

This is why many people choose a Roth IRA as a healthcare savings vehicle instead.

ROTH IRA

The Roth version of the IRA allows you to put money that has already been taxed into the account, where it grows and may be withdrawn tax-free. Unlike its traditional IRA counterpart, there is no upfront tax deduction on contributions. However, as long as you hold onto the account for at least five years and are no younger than fifty-nine and a half when you withdraw your funds, there is no penalty for withdrawals, and they can be used for anything—including medical expenses. In addition, if you enjoy perfect health throughout your retirement and find that you do not need to touch the money you have set aside in the Roth IRA you opened for that purpose, there is no mandatory withdrawal, as there is with a traditional IRA.

One final advantage to Roth IRAs is the relatively high contribution limit. The general contribution limit for 2015 is $5,500, while those who are fifty or older may contribute an additional $1,000.

Limits on IRAs

Please note that the limits mentioned are an aggregate of what you can contribute to all of your IRAs if you hold more than one. However, the IRA limits are *not* related to the limits on contributions to either 401(k) plans or HSAs.

Investing in a Roth IRA will provide you with tax-free money that you can access for any needs (medical or otherwise) as soon as you've reached the five-year/age fifty-nine-and-a-half milestone. Though you do not get the full tax advantages offered to those investing in an HSA, the Roth IRA is probably a better bet since you will not be scrambling if you get seriously ill before you reach retirement.

Medicare Covers Less (and Costs More) Than You Think

Some of the most common myths about American retirement concern Medicare. From confusion about whether or not enrollment is automatic to the belief that the program is entirely free for those enrolled, I have heard more individuals state misconceptions as fact about Medicare than about any other aspect of retirement.

However, the most damaging beliefs about Medicare stem from misunderstandings about what it covers. Let's take a look at the coverage offered by Original Medicare, a.k.a. Medicare Parts A and B.

MEDICARE PART A COVERAGE

Part A is also known as hospital insurance, and in short, it (partially) covers:

- Inpatient hospital care
- Inpatient care in a skilled nursing facility
- Home healthcare
- Hospice care

If you need to stay in a hospital, if you need skilled nursing care (after certain other obligations have been met) either in a facility or at home, or if you need hospice care, then Medicare Part A will cover some portion of your care for each benefit period. (A benefit period is defined as the period of time that you spend in a hospital or skilled nursing facility due to a particular illness or injury, and it lasts until you have been out of the hospital for sixty consecutive days.)

This is the breakdown of what Medicare Part A covers.

Hospital Care

1. *The Deductible:* For each benefit period that you use, you must pay a deductible before the Medicare coverage kicks in. As of 2015, this deductible is $1,260.

2. *Your First Sixty Days in the Hospital:* After you have reached the benefit period deductible, Medicare covers 100 percent of your inpatient care for the first sixty days that you spend in a hospital. This coverage includes a semi-private room, meals, general nursing and doctor care, and drugs administered in the hospital. Medicare does not cover a private room (unless a doctor has deemed it medically necessary), private-duty nursing, or a television or phone in your room if the hospital charges separately for these items.

   An overnight stay in a hospital does not necessarily mean that you are an inpatient and therefore covered by Medicare. You are only considered an inpatient once a doctor has formally admitted you to the hospital.

3. *Days Sixty-One Through Ninety:* If your stay in the hospital stretches past sixty days for a single benefit period, Medicare no longer picks up 100 percent of the tab for your care. For days sixty-one through ninety, you must pay a coinsurance amount, while Medicare pays for the remainder. As of 2015, that coinsurance amount is $315 per day, although the price goes up each year.

4. *Reserve Days:* Once you have spent ninety days in the hospital during a single benefit period, you have reached the end of what Medicare covers. However, you do have what's known as "lifetime reserve days." These are additional days that Medicare will help pay for when you have stayed in the hospital past ninety days during a particular benefit period. Each beneficiary has a total of sixty reserve days to use in his lifetime. There is a coinsurance amount—$630 per reserve day as of 2015—that you

must pay in order to use your reserve days. You do not have to use all of these reserve days during one benefit period, but once you have used any reserve days, they are gone forever.

5. *More Than 150 Days in the Hospital:* If you end up staying in the hospital for more than 150 days during a particular benefit period, you exhaust your Medicare benefits and will then be on the hook for all the costs for each additional day you spend in the hospital.

However, once you have been out of the hospital for at least sixty days, a return to the hospital will at that point be considered a different benefit period, meaning that you will again be covered for your care.

Skilled Nursing Facility Care

The most common misconception about Medicare is that the program covers a stay in a nursing home. Unfortunately, the reality is that you are covered for only a limited amount of skilled nursing care on an inpatient basis. The operative word here is "skilled." That means that any kind of long-term care you need that does not specifically require medical knowledge—help with daily activities like bathing, dressing, eating, walking, etc.—is not covered by Medicare.

Medicare covers your stay in a skilled nursing facility after you have spent a minimum of three days as an inpatient in the hospital for medically necessary reasons—and the length of your inpatient stay does not include the day that you are discharged. Your doctor must also certify that you need daily skilled care, such as intravenous injections or physical therapy, in order for you to qualify for Medicare benefits.

Medicare covers semi-private rooms, meals, and skilled nursing and rehabilitative services in a skilled nursing facility. As with hospital coverage, Medicare won't pay for you to have a private room or a telephone or television in your room.

Here's what's covered:

1. *Your First Twenty Days in a Skilled Nursing Facility:* Medicare covers all costs for your first twenty days in such a facility, provided you meet the stated requirements.

2. *Days Twenty-One Through 100:* After your first twenty days, Medicare requires you to pay a coinsurance amount for each day of your care. As of 2015, that amount is $157.50 per day.

3. *More Than 100 Days of Care:* After you have stayed for 100 days in a skilled nursing facility, you have exhausted your Medicare benefits for that benefit period. (As with hospital stays, if you end up having to return to a skilled nursing facility during a different benefit period, Medicare will kick in again and pay for that care.) Unlike Medicare-covered hospital stays, you cannot use reserve days during a stay at a skilled nursing facility, so you must pay for all costs after reaching day 100 in a benefit period.

Home Healthcare

In order to qualify for home healthcare, you must be homebound, you must have a doctor's order for specific types of healthcare within your home, and you must receive your care from a Medicare-certified home healthcare agency.

Those types of healthcare that qualify for Medicare coverage include medically necessary skilled nursing care (either part-time or intermittent, but not round-the-clock), physical and occupational therapy, and speech-language or pathology services.

Medicare pays 100 percent of these covered services. However, you will have to pay 20 percent of the Medicare-approved amount for any durable medical equipment (such as walkers, hospital beds, etc.) that you may need for your home healthcare.

Hospice Care

This is one situation where Medicare covers 100 percent of the charges (with two exceptions). In order to qualify, your doctor must have given you a diagnosis of a terminal illness and a prognosis of six months or less.

If you defy the odds, Medicare will continue to cover your hospice care for as long as your doctor feels that the case is terminal. There is no limit to the amount of hospice care that you may receive through Medicare.

The two exceptions to the 100 percent payment rule are for prescription drugs for pain and symptom management that are administered at home, and for respite care. Medicare requires that you pay up to a $5 copayment for each prescription administered at home, and for 5 percent of any inpatient care you receive for up to five days in order to give your primary caretakers a respite.

MEDICARE PART B COVERAGE

For the most part, Medicare Part B works much like the typical health insurance you have been familiar with throughout your life. For instance, unlike Medicare Part A, all enrollees in Medicare Part B are required to pay a monthly premium for the program, which is currently set at $104.90. In addition, with Part B, you will pay all costs for covered services until you reach the annual deductible of $147. Once you have met the deductible, you will typically pay 20 percent of the Medicare-approved amount for any particular service.

Medicare Part B is intended to help patients pay for the types of medical care and treatment you receive outside of a hospital. In short, this program covers services from doctors and other healthcare providers, outpatient care, home healthcare, durable medical equipment, and some preventive care. When coupled with Medicare Part A, Part B can help beneficiaries pay for the majority of medical treatments a senior might need. Unfortunately, there is no annual limit on how much you will have to pay out of pocket through Part B, and it can be surprisingly expensive. (For a full list of services covered by Medicare Part B, visit *www.medicare.gov/Pubs/pdf/10050.pdf*.)

It is important to note the coverage gaps within Medicare Part B, because they often take retirees by surprise. In particular, Part B does not cover:

- Long-term care, also known as custodial care (non-medical help that the elderly might need for daily living)

- Self-administered prescription drugs (i.e., any prescriptions you take at home that you do not need a doctor or nurse to administer)
- Routine dental or eye care
- Dentures
- Cosmetic surgery
- Acupuncture
- Hearing aids and the exams for fitting them
- Routine foot care

Long-term care is a major coverage gap, as costs for such care can devastate a retirement income. Savvy retirees plan ahead for this gap, recognizing that long-term care insurance could be a good way to protect themselves.

Long-Term Care Insurance

The gap in long-term care insurance is truly frightening when you realize just how many individuals are affected: Penelope Wang of *Time* magazine reports that 70 percent of individuals over the age of sixty-five will need long-term care in some form. Neither Medicare nor private health insurance covers the sort of non-medical daily living care that many elderly individuals need—which includes help with eating, bathing, dressing, and mobility.

All of that care is expensive. The Genworth 2014 Cost of Care Survey found that the average nursing home costs $77,000 per year (or about $212 per day), and the average nursing home stay is just under three years. In-home care is cheaper but still costs an average of $20 per hour.

The good news is that the Center for Retirement Research at Boston College has found that the financial risks of long-term care may have been overstated. That's because most individuals will typically transition through levels of care. You might start off living independently, find that you need help around the house after a bad fall, need to move into a nursing home after a stroke, and return to independent living again once you recover. Previous analysis of long-term care needs have not necessarily taken these transitional stages into account.

However, it's important to remember that some individuals who need long-term care—such as those afflicted with dementia or Alzheimer's—are otherwise perfectly healthy and could live a long life while needing daily assistance. So it's important to plan ahead for the possibility of long-term care.

Long-term care insurance is often the best option for middle-income retirees. Wealthy individuals can afford to pay out of pocket for their long-term care needs. Those with limited assets are eligible for Medicaid, which does pay for long-term care—but limited assets truly means limited. The guideline is that the person needing care cannot have more than $2,000 in his or her own name. Most middle-income retirees would have to completely exhaust their own resources before being able to qualify for help from Medicaid. (And no transferring your assets to a loved one in order to meet the poverty guidelines—the government's onto that.)

Long-Term Care Insurance Costs

Unfortunately, long-term care insurance is not cheap. As of 2012, the average annual cost to insure a sixty-year-old couple is $3,381 combined, with a benefit of $164,000 each (or $328,000 combined). Unlike health insurance, where the insurance company directly pays the caregiver, long-term care insurance generally requires the policyholder to pay out of pocket for the care and then submit proof of service in order to be reimbursed. In addition, there is usually an elimination period that can span anywhere from twenty to 120 days, during which time you're entirely on the hook for expenses.

There are ways to reduce the costs of long-term care insurance. For instance, while it is possible to purchase a long-term care insurance policy that covers any contingency, those premiums will often be out of reach for the average retiree. Instead, it's important to choose the policy that will best protect you—and to make plans with that policy in mind.

In particular, increasing the elimination period can make your premiums more affordable. However, you will need to know how you can afford that gap in coverage. It pays to have some sort of emergency fund set aside for long-term care. This will give you the ready cash to pay for your elimination period, as well as for the care you receive before you are reimbursed by the insurance company.

In addition, lowering your benefits can help to keep your policy affordable. For instance, the typical length of a nursing home stay is less than three years. Many policyholders will opt for the insurance that only covers up to three years worth of nursing-home care, rather than an indefinite stay, in order to save on their premiums.

There are, however, two features that you should make sure are included in your policy. The first is inflation protection, which will ensure that the care you are buying for yourself now will keep pace with rising healthcare costs. The second is a waiver-of-premium benefit, which will allow you to suspend your premium payments once you are eligible for benefits.

Long-term care insurance is not necessarily the right choice for every retiree. According to the study from the Center for Retirement Research at Boston College, this type of insurance only will only be a good financial decision for about 20 percent of retirees. For most people, it makes better financial sense to spend down their assets until they are eligible for Medicaid. Unless you have good reason to believe that you will need extensive long-term care in your old age—because of a family history of Alzheimer's, for instance—long-term care insurance might not be the right product for you. The important thing is to explore your financial options and have a plan in place for long-term care well before you need it.

Chapter 7 Takeaways

1. The average sixty-five-year-old couple retiring in 2014 will need $220,000 in current dollars to cover their healthcare costs in retirement.

2. Health Savings Accounts (HSA) allow you to put aside pre-tax money for future healthcare costs, making them one possible option for preparing for healthcare in retirement. However, in order to qualify for an HSA, you must be signed up for a high-deductible health plan—which can end up being very costly if you get sick before you retire.

3. Money set aside in a Roth IRA can be used for any purpose, including healthcare costs, provided you have held the account for at least five years and are making withdrawals after you have reached age fifty-nine and a half.

4. Seventy percent of retirees will require some type of long-term care. The average cost for such care is $77,000 per year for nursing-home care, and $20 per hour for in-home care.

5. Long-term care insurance will make good financial sense for about 20 percent of retirees. For many others, it will make more sense to exhaust their assets in order to become eligible for Medicaid. No matter what your financial situation, it's important to plan for how you will handle your long-term care needs.

PART III

Dream Big

Here's where the rubber hits the road, where you figure out what your retirement path is going to look
like. Sure, you may not necessarily be able to pass your
golden years living in a chateau in Napa Valley wine
country, but if you've been following my instructions
and giving careful thought to your planning, you can
have a lot of options for retirement.

How to Retire in Place

WHAT YOU'LL LEARN IN THIS CHAPTER

This chapter will walk you through the most basic option for retirement: staying right where you are when you retire on the conventional timeline. Just because this is the most straightforward retirement option, however, does not mean that it lacks complexity. In this chapter, you will learn the fundamentals of retirement budgeting. You will understand what housing issues to consider as you look toward retirement. You will learn how Medicare can affect your healthcare choices in retirement. Finally, you will take the time to plan for the unique psychological issues you can expect as you transition to the next chapter in your life.

Budgeting While Retired

Budgeting is one of those deceptively straightforward skills that can be out of reach for even the smartest and savviest of individuals. That's because the basic idea behind budgeting—ensuring that you spend less than your income—is simple but not easy. Just because we all know what we should be doing with our money does not make doing it a walk in the park.

In addition, successful budgeting requires your budget to be a living document that changes with your circumstances. This aspect of budgeting is often neglected, even if you have taken the time to create a budget in the first place.

These difficulties inherent in household budgeting are why it is so important to create a retirement budget. Not only can living on a fixed retirement income make budgeting oopsies into huge problems, but retiring without a framework for spending can lead to disordered financial behavior, such as overspending early on and running out of money, or living like a pauper when you're sitting on a sizeable portfolio.

Working through this section will help you to create an initial retirement budget, which you will be able to tweak and maintain throughout your retirement. Let's start with calculating your known retirement income in Worksheet 8-1.

Look up the amount of money you can count on from any pensions you may have and from Social Security. (You can use the Social Security Administration's benefit estimator at *www.socialsecurity.gov/estimator* in order to get a rough idea of how much to expect in retirement.)

WORKSHEET 8-1:
Guaranteed Income

CATEGORY	MONTHLY BENEFIT	MULTIPLY BY 12	ANNUAL AMOUNT
Pension(s):		x 12	
Social Security:		x 12	
TOTAL:		x 12	

In addition to your guaranteed monthly income, you should calculate how much your retirement investment vehicles will generate for you in retirement. The formula for calculating compound interest plus your annual savings is too complex to reproduce here, but there are several excellent calculators available online to do this math for you. In particular, Vanguard's Retirement Income Calculator (*https://retirementplans. vanguard.com/VGApp/pe/pubeducation/calculators/RetirementIncomeCalc.jsf*) offers you the ability to see what kind of monthly income you can expect based upon your years to retirement, the current size of your nest egg, the amount you put away annually, and your expected interest on your investments. (The calculator also offers you the choice of including or excluding your Social Security and pension income, so be sure you do not count that income more than once.) Vanguard's calculator provides you a monthly income number, which means you will need to multiply it by twelve to determine your yearly income.

WORKSHEET 8-2:
Retirement Investment Income

VANGUARD'S MONTHLY INCOME CALCULATION	MULTIPLY BY 12	ANNUAL INVESTMENT INCOME
	x 12	

Now that you have a basic idea of what your annual income in retirement will be, let's revisit your retirement expenses, which you calculated in Worksheet 5-1 in Chapter 5:

WORKSHEET 5-1
Calculating Basic Retirement Expenses

CATEGORY	COST
Rent/mortgage:	
Car payment:	
Groceries and household items:	
Dining out:	
Gasoline:	
Public transportation:	
Electric bill:	
Gas bill:	
Water bill:	
Trash pickup bill:	
Cable/Internet/satellite bill:	
Telephone bill:	
Cell phone bill:	

Credit card/loan payments:

Personal care (haircuts, etc.):

Health/dental insurance:

Subscriptions:

Memberships:

Property taxes:

Homeowners insurance:

Car insurance:

Miscellaneous:

TOTAL:

Now multiply that number by twelve in order to determine your yearly retirement expenses:

$$\text{......................} \times 12 = \text{......................}$$

From here, you can decide if your projected retirement budget is balanced through simple subtraction:

Is Your Retirement Budget Balanced?

Pension and Social Security Income	$
Investment Income	+ $
Expenses	– $
Balance	= $

Unfortunately, even if you have a large positive number as your balance, you are not quite done calculating your retirement budget. That's because there are aspects of retirement that are both cheaper and more expensive than career living. It's important to incorporate both your anticipated retirement savings and retirement expenses into your post-career budget. Worksheets 8-4, 8-5, and 8-6 will walk you through these calculations.

WORKSHEET 8-4: ANTICIPATED RETIREMENT SAVINGS

To calculate your savings regarding car costs, you will have to do a little math prior to filling in the following table. If you can sell your car, then you will need to calculate your monthly savings on your car payment, insurance, gasoline, and maintenance, add them together, and multiply by twelve in order to find your yearly savings:

Car Savings When Selling a Car at Retirement

Car Payment +	Insurance +	Gasoline +	Maintenance*	x 12	= Yearly Savings
				x 12 =	

*Car maintenance is one of the most difficult budget items to calculate. If you are not sure how much your car costs in maintenance, the True Cost to Own calculator on Edmunds.com is an excellent resource (*www.edmunds.com/tco.html*).

If you plan on keeping your car, however, you can still potentially save money on your car expenses after you retire. Figure out how many miles you drive per day for work. Make sure that you include any driving you might do to get to and from lunch in your mileage calculation. Then multiply that number by 250, which is the typical number of days a full-time employee works per year (at five days per week for fifty weeks out of the year). Once you have your yearly work-related mileage, multiply the mileage by 57.5 cents (the IRS deductible mileage expense for 2015, and generally accepted as the amount it costs to drive per mile).

Car Savings When No Longer Driving to Work

Miles per Day	x 250	= Miles per Year	x $0.575	= Yearly Savings
	x 250	=	x $0.575	=

Now you're ready to calculate how much you'll save by not working:

WORKSHEET 8-4:

Anticipated Savings from Retirement

Expense	How Much You Currently Spend per Month Because You Work	Multiply By	Annual Savings
Car		x 12	
Clothing		x 12	
Dining out		x 12	
Dry cleaning		x 12	
Tolls/parking		x 12	
Public transportation		x 12	
Personal care		x 12	
Convenience purchases*		x 12	
Professional services**		x 12	
Stress relief***		x 12	
Professional subscriptions or tools		x 12	
Conference costs		x 12	
Other expenditures		x 12	
TOTAL		x 12	

*Convenience purchases include everything from the convenience foods you rely on because you have little time for cooking while working to the purchases you make without shopping around because of time constraints.

**Professional services can include house cleaners, lawn care, painters, professional drivers/airport shuttles (if you travel a great deal for work, for example), and other services that you will take care of yourself in retirement.

***Stress relief can include things like massages, spa treatments, chiropractors, and other self-care that you use in order to relieve the stress of working that you will no longer need in retirement.

After making those calculations, you might be forgiven for thinking that employment is far more expensive than retirement. However, these calculations don't take into account what you will doing with your time when you're no longer spending forty hours a week working. As a retiree, you might spend more money on travel and hobbies than you did as a worker, which might eat up quite a bit of those savings.

WORKSHEET 8-5:
Anticipated Retirement-Related Expenses

EXPENSE	AMOUNT	MULTIPLY BY	ANNUAL AMOUNT
Hobbies		x 12	
Memberships (including country clubs)		x 12	
Local travel		x 12	
Mortgage for vacation home		x 12	
Holiday/family travel*		x 4	
Vacation travel		x 1	
TOTAL			

*Depending on where you and your extended family lives, you may travel to see family more or less often than quarterly. Adjust these calculations according to your specific circumstances.

In addition to the retirement expenses you can expect, it is also smart to plan for the big one-time expenses in your retirement budget. You will still have to maintain and replace your durable goods in retirement, and you will no longer have an income that can easily take a one-time hit if you forget to plan ahead for these purchases. Worksheet 8-6, adapted from Henry K. "Bud" Hebeler's Replacement Budgeting Worksheet on his website Analyze Now (*www.analyzenow.com*), will help you make these calculations.

WORKSHEET 8-6:

Budgeting for Replacement Expenses

ITEM	COST TO REPLACE	ESTI-MATED LIFE IN YEARS	CURRENT AGE	COST/ YEAR (Cost to Replace/ Estimated Life)	UNITS TO BUY ([30 Years of Retirement + Current Age of Item] /Estimated Life)	TOTAL AMOUNT TO SAVE (Cost to Replace × Units to Buy)
Car 1		8				
Car 2		8				
Replace roof		25				
Exterior paint		10				
Large-screen TV		7				
Furnace		20				
Carpet		15				
Air conditioning		10				
Interior paint		5				
Drapes		15				
Computer		5				
Freezer		20				
Hot water heater		10				
Dishwasher		15				
Refrigerator		20				
Washing machine		15				
Dryer		15				

Mattress	10				
Exercise equipment	15				
TOTALS			YEARLY TOTAL		RETIRE-MENT TOTAL

The yearly total is the amount you will need to have set aside from your yearly budget to be prepared for these replacements costs. The retirement total is the amount you will need to have set aside within your nest egg in order to cover all the replacement costs you will see throughout your retirement

Using the information from Worksheets 8-4, 8-5, and 8-6, you can determine if the amount of money you save by not working will offset the anticipated expenses of your retirement activities and your replacement expenses for durable goods in retirement:

WORKSHEET 8-7:
Spending More or Spending Less in Retirement?

Retirement Savings	$
Retirement Expenses	– $
Replacement Expenses	– $
Balance	= $

If you have found that all of these calculations still leave you in the red, there are two things you can do to balance your retirement budget:

1. Increase your savings rate

2. Reduce your expenses

The benefit of calculating a retirement budget in advance of your projected retirement date is that it gives you the opportunity to up your savings while you still have time. And while it is *always* possible to reduce your expenses, knowing ahead of time that your expensive retirement plans might need some tweaking can help you to psychologically prepare for the retirement you can afford.

Housing Issues in Retirement

By the end of this section, you will have a plan in place for housing costs, maintenance issues, and mobility as you prepare your current home to become your cozy retirement retreat.

THE COST OF STAYING HOME

Even if you have paid off your mortgage prior to retirement, your house can still take a big bite out of your monthly retirement income. Worksheet 8-8 will help you calculate how much it will cost you to stay put.

For the Love of Pete, Pay Off Your Mortgage Before You Retire!

Having your mortgage paid off means lower monthly expenses, a lower tax burden if you are paying your mortgage using IRA or 401(k) withdrawals, and it means you have an additional large asset in your portfolio that you own free and clear. Do not add to your retirement expenses (and headaches!) unnecessarily by retiring before you have paid off your mortgage.

WORKSHEET 8-8:

The Yearly Costs of Staying in Your Current Home

EXPENSE	AMOUNT
Mortgage	
Property taxes	
Homeowners insurance	
Home maintenance*	
TOTAL	

*You can use the replacement costs figure from Worksheet 8-6 (minus car replacement) for this calculation.

An additional consideration you will need to potentially add into your calculations is the cost of making accommodations for reduced mobility as you age. This cost will depend entirely on your specific circumstances: how your mobility is specifically affected and how your home is already set up. However, HomeAdvisor (*www.homeadvisor.com*), a website that helps homeowners determine the costs of various home improvements, calculates that the average cost to remodel for disability accommodation is nearly $9,000, and can be as high as $20,000.

TAPPING INTO YOUR EQUITY WITH A REVERSE MORTGAGE

If this is the first time you have calculated the specific costs of staying put, it may seem as though continuing to live in your current home is more expensive than it is worth. However, one potential benefit of staying put in retirement is the fact that you have the option of taking a reverse mortgage.

While reverse mortgages are not always a smart financial choice, they can provide retirees who are staying in their homes with a way to tap the equity in one of their largest assets. Here's how a reverse mortgage works.

Reverse Mortgage Basics

A reverse mortgage is one of the few banking terms that is just what it sounds like. Instead of borrowing money from the bank that you will have to pay off in installments, the bank lets you tap the equity in the home you own, generally either in a lump sum or in installments, while you live there. You owe closing costs at the time you take the reverse mortgage, and you will be accruing interest throughout the life of the reverse mortgage, which will have to be paid back along with the loan balance at the end of the term. (However, that term does not end until you move permanently, sell the house, or pass away.)

In order to qualify for a reverse mortgage, you must meet several requirements:

- You and your spouse must both be over age sixty-two.
- You must own your home and have a significant amount of equity in it if your mortgage is not entirely paid off. (If you still have a mortgage, you must use the proceeds from the reverse mortgage to pay it off.)
- You must live in the home full-time.

If you meet these requirements, the amount that you are eligible to borrow depends on a number of factors, including your (and your spouse's) age, the appraised value of your home, and current interest rates. The older the youngest borrower is, the more equity you have in your home, and the lower the interest rate, the more cash you can get out of a reverse mortgage. However, there is a limit of $625,500 on reverse mortgage lending, no matter what the appraised value of the home.

There are a few ways that you can receive your payments from a reverse mortgage:

- As a lump sum. This option has the highest level of interest and fees.
- In monthly installments. You can either choose to receive your payments for a fixed term or for life—which, if you are a co-owner with your spouse, means for the life of both spouses.

- As a line of credit, which can be withdrawn as needed. This option will maximize the amount of money available to you for withdrawal.
- Through some combination of the first three options.

One more advantage of the reverse mortgage is the fact that your payments are entirely tax-free and will generally not affect your Social Security or Medicare benefits. (However, if you do qualify for low-income assistance from the government, such as Medicaid, you may find that the money from your reverse mortgage disqualifies you from such benefits.)

Reverse Mortgage Costs

Reverse mortgage lenders protect themselves from the volatility of home value by slapping high origination fees and mortgage insurance on these products. If you are interested in a reverse mortgage, you can expect to pay the following fees:

- An origination fee of 2 percent of the first $200,000 of your home's value, plus another 1 percent for amounts above that, with a cap of $6,000 total for the origination fee.
- An upfront mortgage insurance premium of 2 percent of the home's value.
- An annual mortgage insurance premium of 1.25 percent of the mortgage balance. This amount will go up each year if you are taking installments.
- A monthly servicing charge of up to $35, which gets added on to your loan balance each month.
- Traditional closing costs.

In most cases, retirees who are taking on a reverse mortgage use the proceeds of the loan in order to pay these costs, meaning they will have no out-of-pocket expenses. However, no out-of-pocket expenses does not mean there are no costs.

To start, it's important to remember that there are several ways your loan can come due:

- If you sell the house.
- If you and your spouse die.
- If you can no longer consider your home a primary residence. This goes into effect if you find yourself needing long-term nursing-home care for more than twelve months. Up to that twelve-month limit, you can still consider your home a primary residence.
- Since you continue to hold the title to your house, you could be considered in default on the loan if you do not pay your property taxes, do not have adequate homeowner's insurance, or you fail to maintain your home, at which point your loan would become due.

All of this means a reverse mortgage can add an additional layer of stress to your retirement finances if your health takes a downturn. Losing the ability to care for the house yourself or needing nursing-home care could put you in a position where you will have to sell your house in order to pay off your loan.

Even if everything goes as planned and you stay sharp as a tack and twice as bright until you pass away, a reverse mortgage could leave your heirs in a sticky situation if you wanted to keep your house in the family. Your children would need to have enough cash on hand to be able to pay off the reverse mortgage at the time of your death—otherwise, the bank will sell the house. If there is any equity left, it will go to your family, but depending on how long you have held the reverse mortgage, the sale could leave your heirs with absolutely nothing. In addition, if the loan balance is greater than the value of the home, your children would still have to pay off the full amount of the loan in order to retain ownership.

One final cost to consider is the interest rate on your reverse mortgage. While these rates can be either fixed or variable, you are more likely to be offered a product with a variable rate—making the payoff amount even higher when the loan comes due.

Where to Learn More about Reverse Mortgages

If you are interested in a reverse mortgage, the best choice is through the HUD program called Home Equity Conversion Mortgage (HECM). You can learn more about your options with HECM by calling 1-800-569-4287 or visiting *http://portal.hud.gov/hudportal/ HUD?src=/program_offices/housing/sfh/hecm/hecmabout.*

MOBILITY AND MAINTENANCE

Taking care of and living comfortably in your home are easy to take for granted when you are young. Currently, you might not think twice about mounting a ladder to clean out your gutters each year or climbing stairs when you go to bed each night. But these simple exercises can become hazardous for a retiree who is not as steady on her feet—even if there are no other underlying health issues.

No one can decide for you if your home will become too difficult to maintain and live in. However, it's smart to spend time prior to retirement thinking through the potential problems of staying in your current home as you age. Worksheet 8-9 provides a list of questions to answer to help you determine if and how your current home can meet your needs far into your retirement.

WORKSHEET 8-9: MOBILITY AND MAINTENANCE QUESTIONS TO CONSIDER

1. Do you have reason to believe that you or your spouse's health will deteriorate? ....

2. Will you or your spouse be able to stay independently in your home if the other one passes away? ....

3. What aspects of your home might be difficult to navigate as you age in place? How will you deal with them? ....

....

....

4. How might you be able to rearrange the way you use your home to accommodate mobility issues? For instance, would you be able to set up a master bedroom on the ground floor if stairs become an issue? ....

....

....

5. What maintenance issues do you take care of yourself? What will you do if you can no longer manage those tasks? ....

....

....

6. If you need to stop driving, how will you get around? ....

....

7. What kind of support network do you have in place within your community? ....

....

....

8. How easy or difficult is it for family or friends to visit? ....

....

9. Is it important (to you or to them) that your children inherit your house? (This is an important question to discuss, as your kids might not care as much as you assume they do.) ....

....

Why You Might Consider Downsizing

Even if you decide to retire "in place," downsizing may still be the best option for your housing needs in retirement. Downsizing can offer you the following benefits:

- Reduction in your property taxes
- Reduction of utility costs
- Reduction of maintenance costs (or reduction of time spent on maintenance)
- The ability to access the equity in your home—and if you make a profit on the sale of your home, you will pay no capital gains tax on it unless the profit is greater than $250,000 for a single filer or $500,000 for a married couple
- The psychological benefits of purging and starting anew

Healthcare Issues to Consider

Whether you relocate or stay put in retirement, navigating Medicare is not an easy prospect. Here's what you need to know about staying healthy at home once you are a Medicare beneficiary.

ENROLLING IN MEDICARE

The rules for enrolling in Medicare vary depending on your circumstances, which can lead to a great deal of confusion among potential beneficiaries. Unfortunately, missing an enrollment deadline can be costly, so it's important to make sure you're aware of what you need to do to sign up for Medicare Parts A and B.

Automatic Enrollment

Some Medicare beneficiaries will be automatically enrolled in the program. There are three reasons why you might find yourself receiving a Medicare Part A and Part B card in the mail without having to enroll:

1. You are already receiving Social Security benefits or Railroad Retirement Board benefits. For these individuals, Medicare Parts A and B will automatically kick in on the first day of the month that you turn sixty-five—unless your birthday is on the first of the month, in which case your benefits begin on the first day of the month prior to your sixty-fifth birthday.

2. You are under sixty-five, disabled, and have been receiving Social Security disability benefits for twenty-four months. At that point, you become automatically eligible for and enrolled in Medicare Parts A and B.

3. You have ALS (amyotrophic lateral sclerosis, more commonly called Lou Gehrig's disease). You will be automatically enrolled in Medicare Parts A and B in the same month that your Social Security disability benefits begin.

As you'll recall from Chapter 7, however, Medicare Part B is not premium-free, which means being automatically enrolled in Medicare in this way requires you to start paying the monthly premiums. While most seniors find it is to their financial benefit to enroll in Medicare Part B, you may decide that you do not want to take part in that program, even if you are automatically enrolled in it.

Beneficiaries who are automatically enrolled receive their Medicare card in the mail three months before their sixty-fifth birthday, or one month before their twenty-fifth month of Social Security disability benefits. On the back of the card are instructions for declining Part B coverage. Those who decline will need to follow those instructions and return the Medicare card in the mail to avoid being charged for the Part B premiums.

Signing Up for Part A and Part B

If you are nearing your sixty-fifth birthday and do not meet the automatic enrollment requirements, then you will have to sign up for benefits yourself. The following are the three timeframes during which you may sign up for Medicare Parts A and B:

1. The Initial Enrollment Period

This is the best time to enroll in Medicare. The initial enrollment period is a seven-month timeframe that begins three months before the month you turn sixty-five, includes the month that you turn sixty-five, and ends three months after the month you turn sixty-five.

If you enroll in Medicare Parts A and/or B during this enrollment period, then there is no fee or penalty for enrollment. Enrolling during the three months before your sixty-fifth birthday means that you will have Medicare coverage starting on the first day of your birthday month. If you enroll during your birthday month or in the three months that follow, you will have a delayed start date for coverage. So it's best to get the ball rolling with Medicare *before* your sixty-fifth birthday.

2. The General Enrollment Period

If you missed the seven-month initial enrollment period window, you can still sign up. There is a general enrollment period between January 1 and March 31 every year—and signing up during such a general enrollment will mean that your coverage will begin July 1 of that year. However, there is a penalty for missing your initial enrollment period for Medicare Part B. You will have to pay the late enrollment penalty for as long as you are a Medicare beneficiary. The monthly premium will go up by 10 percent for each full twelve-month period that you were eligible for Part B but did not sign up.

3. The Special Enrollment Period

This period is for those beneficiaries who were covered under a group health plan through either their own or their spouse's employment when they turned sixty-five. Those potential beneficiaries who already have health insurance as of their sixty-fifth birthday are not required to sign up for Medicare during their initial enrollment period—although they are encouraged to do so.

Medicare will allow such double-covered beneficiaries to enroll at any time when they are still covered by their group health plan, or during the eight-month period that begins the month after either the employment or the health coverage ends—whichever happens first.

FINDING DOCTORS WHO ACCEPT MEDICARE

It may surprise you to learn that not all doctors are willing to accept Medicare (which is known in the program as "accepting assignment"). Doctors who refuse to accept assignment or who refuse to treat Medicare patients altogether generally do so because they do not want to deal with the complexity of the Medicare payment system, which, to be fair, is rather convoluted.

Understanding Medicare Assignment and Medicare-Approved Amounts

Medicare negotiates with doctors and healthcare service providers to set prices for particular services, tests, medical goods, etc. The amount agreed upon by both Medicare and the service provider is known as the Medicare-approved amount. Medicare pays 80 percent of the approved amount to the provider, while the patient owes the remaining 20 percent of the Medicare-approved amount to the doctor as a coinsurance payment. The doctors and healthcare providers who agree to this Medicare-approved amount are referred to as either "accepting assignment" or as "assigned providers," and the payment for treatment from such a doctor should be relatively straightforward.

However, if you are treated by a doctor who does not accept assignment, things get more complicated. At that point, the doctor may charge you for the difference between the Medicare-approved amount and the full amount that she usually charges—up to 15 percent of the Medicare-approved amount. You'll have to pay that amount in addition to the 20 percent coinsurance amount that you already owe for care.

Whether she accepts assignment or not, the doctor treating a Medicare patient is required to accept less money total than she would normally accept from a non-Medicare patient. However, the doctor cannot legally ask for more than 35 percent of the Medicare-approved amount from the patient if the doctor is not assigned.

The issue of Medicare-approved amounts is the reason why you will find some doctors who simply do not treat Medicare patients.

It is a good idea to learn if your current doctor accepts assignment (or if he treats any Medicare patients at all). If you need to find a new doctor who accepts Medicare assignment, the Medicare Physician Compare website at *www.medicare.gov/physiciancompare/search.html* allows you to search for and compare local doctors and practices.

Psychological Issues in Retirement

With the amount of financial planning necessary to pull off a modern retirement, it can be very easy to forget the psychological impact of ending your career. According to a 2012 study by Dr. Elizabeth Mokyr Horner, published in the *Journal of Happiness Studies*, retirees experience a rush of well-being and life satisfaction immediately after retiring, but they then feel a sharp decline in their levels of happiness a few years into retirement.

This letdown is natural. After you have spent years planning for your retirement, you can hardly expect the reality of it to live up to your expectations.

The important thing is to recognize that a decline in happiness is very common, and to plan ahead for the challenges of ending your career. In particular, researchers have found that there are several things you can do to make this transition as smooth and contented as possible. Gradually implement the following changes to weather any potential retirement letdown.

REDEFINE YOURSELF

Ending a long career can leave some people feeling adrift. Figure out what makes you feel fulfilled, and plan to shape your retired life around those feelings of fulfillment. The time to think about this is several years before you retire, not the day after you receive your gold watch from your employer.

VOLUNTEER

Studies have shown that retirees who volunteer report higher levels of life satisfaction and fewer symptoms of depression. Experts theorize that volunteering is good for retirees because it expands their social circles, and increases their feelings of purpose. Giving your time to a cause you care about can improve your sense of contentment.

EXERCISE

Exercise has been proven to lessen symptoms of depression.

LEARN NEW SKILLS

A recent study published in the journal *Psychological Science* showed that seniors who learned a new skill, such as quilting or digital photography, experienced enhanced cognitive function compared to a control group who just enjoyed social time instead of learning.

Chapter 8 Takeaways

1. Plan your retirement budget before you retire, so that you can increase your savings rate or reduce your anticipated expenses before you are stuck on a fixed income.

2. Plan to have your mortgage paid off prior to retirement.

3. A reverse mortgage can offer additional income for a retiree who is aging in place, but you should be cautious about taking one due to the costs associated with them.

4. Think through which aspects of living at home will become difficult as you age.

5. Do not miss enrollment deadlines for Medicare, as late enrollment can be costly.

6. Be sure you understand whether your doctor accepts Medicare assignment prior to retirement.

7. Retirement letdown is a common problem, but redefining yourself, volunteering your time, exercising, and learning new things can all help to smooth the transition to the next chapter of your life.

CHAPTER 9

How to Move Closer to Family in Retirement

WHAT YOU'LL LEARN IN THIS CHAPTER

Retiring closer to your family may be the culmination of a dream, or it may be a practical decision to help you eke out a less-than-robust retirement. In either case, you need to make sure you think through all of the ramifications of relocation. In this chapter, you will learn how to handle the overwhelming task of downsizing before moving. You will walk through the financial considerations of moving—from moving expenses to taxes to cost of living. Finally, you will understand why it is important to manage your own and your family's expectations of your relocation, and you will learn what questions to ask and what plans to put in place to make the transition as smooth as possible.

How to Downsize

There is an excellent reason why psychologists rank moving house as the third most stressful life event, after death of a spouse and divorce. Packing up everything you own, hauling it elsewhere, and then unpacking it is overwhelming. Doing so after living in the same place for years or decades can add to the stress, since it can be almost impossible to determine what to keep and what to discard. Downsizing only gets more difficult as you age; according to a recent study, people become increasingly less likely to get rid of unnecessary possessions after age fifty.

However, divesting yourself of possessions you no longer need is one of the best ways to make the transition to your new home a smooth one. Here is where to start, especially if you feel overwhelmed at the idea of dismantling your home:

A Little at a Time or Rip Off the Band-Aid?

There are two schools of thought when it comes to downsizing. Some experts recommend parting with items slowly, so that you do not feel overwhelmed by the scope of the task. If you follow these experts, then you will start downsizing months (or even a year or more) ahead of your planned move, and you will sell, donate, or throw away a little bit at a time. This can help you to soften the emotional impact of getting rid of your things.

Other experts suggest that purging should be done as quickly as possible. Doing all of your discarding in one shot gives you a profound feeling of freedom and transformation, and prevents you from feeling as though you are slogging through an unending and impossible long-term task.

Either technique will get the job done, and only you can know if slow-and-steady or all-at-once is going to be most effective for you. Either way, it's best to plan on starting your downsizing well in advance of your move.

START WITH A FLOOR PLAN (IF YOU CAN)

You will presumably be moving into a smaller space, so plot out exactly how much room you will have. This will help you to determine what furniture you will need and what will not fit. If you already know where you will be living, take the time to plot out the floor plan on graph paper, and decide where your various furnishings will go. Better to know early on that your grandmother's sideboard can't fit into your new dining room.

Even if you do not know exactly where you will be hanging your hat when you relocate, decide ahead of time what kind of square footage you will be happy with and purge unnecessary furniture accordingly.

CLEAR OUT YOUR CHILDREN'S THINGS

It's likely you are still housing many of your kids' childhood mementos: everything from prom dresses to teddy bears to report cards. It can be difficult for grown children to find the time to sort through these treasures, so let them know that you will be boxing everything up and that you will hold onto the box until a specific date, at which point you will trash it. Do not take on the job of sorting and storing your children's belongings when you have to downsize your own.

DECIDE NOW WHO WILL RECEIVE HEIRLOOMS

If there are any items that you plan to give to family or friends, start making those decisions now—and put it in writing. This can help in two ways: You may decide to gift the heirlooms to your loved ones now, which will help you in your downsizing efforts, and it can help to defuse future stress if more than one family member is interested in the same item.

PURGE IN LESSER-USED ROOMS FIRST

Not only will this focus allow you to keep any clutter out of your main living areas, but items in the rooms you use the least are probably the ones that will be easiest to sort through, since they are often either heirlooms or unnecessary.

WRITE DOWN YOUR MEMORIES

Often, possessions are important because they remind you of an event or a time in your life. If you write down what makes these items special, it can be easier to part with them. You will always have the story—or you can pass the story along to the new owner of the item.

ORGANIZATION MATTERS

Make sure that you have a good system in place for sorting your items. Set aside a specific spot for important keepsakes so that you know where they all are.

In addition, don't forget the importance of labeling everything. This will make sorting much easier for you and any helpers you have.

GIVE YOURSELF TIME

Discarding the items that it took a lifetime to accumulate is an emotional process. You are not just sorting through things—each one is a memory. So make sure you give yourself some time to process the emotions that downsizing will trigger.

Financial Considerations of Relocation

Even if you anticipate that you will ultimately save money by moving, there are several moving-related financial issues that you need to factor into your retirement budget. Let's start with the cost of the move itself.

HOW MUCH DOES IT COST TO RELOCATE?

The average cost of a long-distance move is difficult to pin down, because most long-distance movers calculate their rates based upon the weight and cubic feet of your goods and the distance of the relocation. That being said, Worldwide ERC, an association that tracks the cost of workforce mobility, estimated the average cost of a professional household move in 2012 at $12,459. These costs were calculated for relocations that include full-service movers and no downsizing, which means your move might be less expensive, depending on how much or little you are moving, and whether you are willing to do some or all of the packing and hauling yourself. A full-service mover generally offers packing, hauling, storing (if you cannot move directly into your new home), and unpacking services, so any retiree willing to do some of that work himself will probably spend less than Worldwide ERC estimates.

Suffice it to say, even if you are willing to go the DIY moving route—a prospect that is even less fun in retirement than it was in your youth—you should plan for fairly high relocation costs. The website Moving Guru offers a good calculator for determining the cost of a move at *www.movingguru.com/movingcostcalculator.*

If you decide to use professional movers for any portion of your relocation, you will want to get estimates from multiple companies before deciding on a mover. AARP lists the following tips for finding a reputable professional mover.

Beware Moving Scams

According to the Federal Motor Carrier Safety Administration (FMCSA), the watchdog organization that keeps tabs on interstate moving companies, scam moving companies (known in the industry as "rogue operators") can be a serious problem. You can research the background of any interstate mover, including complaints, safety information, licensing, registration status with the Department of Transportation, and company contact information, on the FMCSA website at *http://ai.fmcsa.dot.gov/hhg/search.asp.*

- Get an in-home estimate. As previously stated, long-distance moving costs are based upon distance and the weight and size of your goods. Offering you a cost estimate sight unseen is a red flag that you should not trust that mover.
- Federal regulations require that all movers provide you with a copy of *Your Rights and Responsibilities When You Move.*
- Your contract with your mover must include exact price estimates, pickup and delivery dates, and insurance amounts.
- Reputable companies do not request upfront payment. You should expect to pay at the time of delivery.

- While it is possible for a moving company to legally make an estimate that is too low, federal law requires movers to complete delivery as long as you pay 110 percent of the estimated price.

MOVING AND TAXES

The weather is not the only reason why Florida is considered a good place to retire: It is also one of a handful of states that have no tax on income. But the calculation for determining your tax burden in a new home is about more than just state income tax. There are four state taxes that you will want to account for as you plan for your life in your new home:

1. Income Tax. There are currently seven states without any income tax: Alaska, Florida, Nevada, South Dakota, Texas, Washington, and Wyoming. In addition, New Hampshire and Tennessee only tax dividends and interest. While moving to one of these nine states could mean that your retirement income will go further, particularly if the majority of your income is derived from tax-deferred accounts like a 401(k) or traditional IRA, it's important to remember that there are other taxes that could take a bite out of your income. For example, while Texas has no income tax, the property taxes in the Lone Star State are high, meaning a move there could mean you are trading one tax for another. Also, Tennessee may only tax dividends and interest, but the combined state and local sales tax rate there is the nation's highest at 9.45 percent.

2. Property Tax. It's important to know how much your new home will cost you in property taxes, as well as if there are any local exemptions, credits, or rebates for senior homeowners.

3. Sales Tax. Five states have no sales tax whatsoever: Alaska, Delaware, Montana, New Hampshire, and Oregon. The other forty-five states (and the District of Columbia) levy taxes at rates

between 2.9 percent (Colorado) and 7.5 percent (California) on the sale of goods, and thirty-eight of those states also have local sales taxes added to the state tax.

4. Taxes on Social Security Benefits. We discussed the complexities of federal taxes on Social Security benefits in Chapter 8—but state taxes on Social Security add another layer. Twelve states tax Social Security income, although some of these states with Social Security income taxes offer exemptions based upon adjusted gross income (AGI) or up to a certain level of income: Colorado, Connecticut, Kansas, Minnesota, Missouri, Montana, Nebraska, New Mexico, North Dakota, Rhode Island, Vermont, and West Virginia.

Considering the additional new taxes you may be facing, as well as new exemptions that you may be eligible for once you move (or age past a particular date), it is a good idea to consult with a tax professional in order to determine exactly how taxes will affect your retirement.

COST OF LIVING

Since your family lives in the area where you plan to move, you may already have a sense of how much it costs to live there. However, it is a good idea to determine exactly how far your retirement income will go in your new home prior to moving there.

CNN Money offers an excellent cost-of-living calculator at *http:// money.cnn.com/calculator/pf/cost-of-living*, which allows you to enter your income, your current city, and your destination city. It then tells you how much more (or less) you will need to maintain your standard of living, with the explicit price differential for groceries, housing, utilities, transportation, and healthcare.

Managing Expectations

Moving closer to family is not just a matter of finances and logistics. You must also consider what impact it will have on your relationships.

While you might have a vision of a Norman Rockwell–style dinner table crowded with cheerful parents, beaming children, and grandchildren to whom you are moving closer, the reality may be a little more like the strained relationships in television's *Everybody Loves Raymond*. The difference often comes down to expectations: What are you hoping your relationships with your now local family will look like, and how do your hopes and expectations compare with those of your family?

It may be uncomfortable, but it is vital that you and your family talk together before your move to determine exactly what your new roles will be in each other's lives.

Here are six questions you should discuss with your family prior to planning your move closer to them:

1. How often will I see or spend time with my kids or grandkids?

2. What kinds of tasks can I reasonably expect my family to help me with, both specifically in terms of the move itself and once I have gotten settled?

3. What kinds of tasks will my family expect of me (such as babysitting, help with carpooling school-age grandchildren, etc.)?

4. What plans do I have in place to make friends and create a social support system in my new home? Will I have any social outlet other than my family?

5. Do I or my family have any financial expectations of each other as a result of this move?

6. What plans do we have in place in case my health or mobility deteriorates?

Moving in with Family

Some retirees will take moving closer to family one step further and move in with their children. While this can be an ideal situation for the entire family, benefiting everyone within the multigenerational household, it can also create a great deal of stress. If you are planning to move in with a family member in retirement, here are several issues that you will want to think through before you call the moving van.

FINANCES

Will you be financially contributing to the household? It could be worthwhile to put in writing what your contribution will be, so that both you and your family are clear on the expectations. In addition, if you will be living with one of your adult children, it's a good idea to discuss with the entire family what your financial contribution to that child's household (or lack thereof) will mean for the entire family. If necessary, consult with an elder law attorney to hammer out the specifics.

FAMILY DYNAMICS

One of the toughest aspects of moving in with an adult child is the change in family dynamics. You are used to being the parent, but you are now living in a household where you do not make the rules. Talk with your family ahead of time about what is expected of you and other members of the household.

LOGISTICAL CONSIDERATIONS

Is your family member's home set up for your needs? If your family needs to do some renovations to make the space ready for you, who will cover the costs?

If you need assistance now or in the future, who will provide it for you? Is your family equipped to help you if and when you need it, or will they be relying on outside caregivers?

Chapter 9 Takeaways

1. Downsizing is key to stress-free moving.

2. Relocation may not be as expensive as you think.

3. Before relocating, investigate four taxes in the state to which you're moving: income tax, property tax, sales tax, and tax on Social Security earnings.

4. If you're moving closer to family, have a frank discussion with them about how this will impact them.

5. If you're moving in with family, discuss everyone's expectations and responsibilities beforehand.

CHAPTER 10

How to Move Into a Retirement Community

WHAT YOU'LL LEARN IN THIS CHAPTER

Modern retirement communities are nothing like the "homes" of yesteryear, and a vibrant, newly retired resident can look forward to years of maintenance-free living, a large group of peers as neighbors, planned activities or onsite recreation, and potentially some health and/or mobility support. However, it's important to thoroughly research any housing option before you buy in. This chapter will break down the four types of retirement communities you will encounter and the average costs associated with each. You will learn the specific options, costs, and pitfalls of Continuing Care Retirement Communities (CCRC). You will understand the tax breaks that can mitigate the (sometimes) excessive costs of retirement community living. Finally, you will learn what questions you need to ask to determine which community is right for you.

Types of Retirement Communities

Let's start by defining each of the different types of retirement communities you are likely to come across.

1. **55+ Retirement Communities:** These communities are much like any other gated or planned communities, except that they

are age-restricted. In general, you will own your home in such a community, which could be anything from a condo to a vacation-style house to an apartment in a high-rise building. Costs vary from community to community, but in addition to your purchase price, plan to pay a monthly fee for maintenance, services, and amenities. That fee can range anywhere from a couple of hundred to several thousand dollars per month.

2. **Independent Living Communities:** These are much like age-restricted retirement communities, except that they tend to also offer a large number of activities and amenities, making them more like all-inclusive resorts rather than a simple neighborhood community. Generally, homes in independent living communities are leased, which can make this a good option for anyone who does not want to be tied down. Often meals, transportation, utilities, light housekeeping, and all maintenance are covered by your monthly fee. However, prices are somewhat steep, averaging between $1,500 and $3,500 per month—or higher, depending on where you live. In addition, some independent living communities charge buy-in fees or also ask you to purchase your home in addition to paying monthly fees.

3. **Assisted Living Facilities:** This option is for retirees with some health issues but who do not need skilled nursing facility care. Your rent pays for a private room, along with access to activities and amenities, meals (in some facilities), and access to skilled nursing and medical care onsite. According to the Genworth 2014 Cost of Care Survey, the monthly payment for an assisted living one-bedroom single occupancy ranges from $750 to $10,412, depending on location, with a national median of $3,500 per month.

4. **Continuing Care Retirement Communities (CCRC):** These are the one-stop-shop of retirement communities, and they can take care of seniors for the rest of their lives. CCRCs offer residents options of independent living, assisted living, and skilled

nursing-home care. As your needs change, you can move from living independently in your own apartment to getting assistance as necessary to receiving skilled nursing care without ever leaving your community. CCRCs require a hefty upfront entrance fee—anywhere from $100,000 to $1 million, although the national average is about $250,000—plus monthly charges that range from $1,000 to $5,000. In addition, those monthly charges may go up if you need to transition from the independent living housing to assisted living or nursing care.

Deciding to move into a 55+ retirement community, an independent living community, or an assisted living facility is fairly straightforward. The contracts and fees you encounter with these types of communities are generally easy to understand (although it is always a good idea to get a second opinion before you sign any legal document), and there are no complex decisions to make before moving in.

CCRCs, on the other hand, are much thornier. Let's take a closer look at these popular retirement communities.

What to Expect from Your CCRC

If you are interested in moving into a community that can potentially serve all of your needs for the rest of your life, a CCRC can be an excellent choice. However, because of the complexity of the CCRC business model—these communities must cater to everyone from relatively young and healthy retirees who want regular tennis lessons to elderly residents who need round-the-clock nursing care—the options and fees available to a potential resident can be very difficult to parse.

CCRC CONTRACT OPTIONS

There are three basic contract options when you move into a CCRC:

1. **Life Care Contract (also called an Extensive Contract):** This option is the most expensive, but your monthly payment does not go up if you have to move into the assisted living or skilled nursing care unit.

2. **Modified Contract:** These contracts offer lower monthly fees, but you are only eligible for a limited use of healthcare services. If your needs exceed your contracted services, then you will have to pay à la carte for additional healthcare services.

3. **Fee-for-Service Contract:** With this option, you lower both your entrance fee (more on that in the next section) and your monthly fee, but you are on the hook for all assisted living and nursing care services at market rates. According to a 2010 Government Accountability Office report, those monthly rates ranged from $4,700 to $6,500 for assisted living and from $8,100 to $10,700 for skilled nursing care.

In addition to having to predict how much healthcare you will need, you must also make certain you fully understand what your rights are according to your contract. Some CCRC facilities write in language that will allow them to involuntarily discharge residents if the retiree either runs out of money or if his need for care becomes too great for the facility to accommodate. These potential issues are one of the many reasons you need to have an independent attorney look through your contract before signing.

CCRC COSTS

As mentioned, new CCRC residents have to pay a large deposit when joining their new home. In most cases, the deposit is either fully or partially refundable, going back to the resident when he moves out or to his estate when he dies. With partially refundable entrance fees—the most common scenario—the size of the refund declines with each month of residency, and the refund ultimately disappears after several years. It's important to note that paying an entrance fee does not mean that you own your independent living unit. The entrance fee simply purchases you the right to live in the community for the rest of your life in accordance with your contract.

If you count on getting your refund back either for yourself or your estate, you should understand the specific rules governing your refund. Most CCRCs do not issue a refund until a new resident has put down her own entrance fee for the unit. If a community is having trouble attracting new residents, you might just be out of luck.

In addition, the monthly costs—which are already fairly steep—can increase annually by 4 percent to 6 percent while you are in the independent living unit, and by even more in the assisted living or nursing care unit. Contracts generally specify that monthly fees are adjustable, so it's a good idea to look into the history of monthly fee increases and ask how the facility decides on such increases. Finally, make sure you know exactly what services you are paying for with your monthly fee and how much additional services will cost, as services can vary widely from one facility to another.

Since monthly fees can change if you move from one unit to another, it's also important to understand how and when you might be transferred. According to Eleanor Laise of Kiplinger, CCRC residents "may feel pressured to move from one level of care to another, such as when a facility says it cannot deliver the required care in an independent-living unit." You may request that your personal physician be involved in any decisions about transferring to another level of care, but you need to be clear on how these decisions will be made. In addition, married couples need to remember that if one spouse moves to another level of care while the other remains in independent living, the community will generally charge you fees for occupying two units.

The Benevolent Fund

Many CCRCs maintain a fund to help out residents who run out of money. The benevolent fund is not anything that a resident should count on, however, and its existence does not necessarily mean that you will be covered in the event that you drain your funds. The availability of the benevolent fund is entirely based on how big it is, under what circumstances it can be used, and how long the CCRC is willing to help a broke resident. Your contract should spell out all of the benevolent fund details.

CCRC PITFALLS

In addition to the complexities of contracts and fees, opting to live in a CRCC is further complicated by the fact that these types of communities are regulated on a state-by-state basis, meaning there is no national oversight or standards across the industry. That leaves potential residents open to some financial pitfalls.

Bankruptcy

The economic downturn hit many of these retirement communities very hard. The CCRC business model is based upon high occupancy, and when the housing market plunged, many potential residents were unable to sell their houses—which is a common strategy for generating the entrance fee. Without maximum occupancy, several communities—including Erickson Retirement Communities, one of the nation's largest CCRC developers—were forced to declare bankruptcy. After such a financial failure, some residents lost their entrance fee refund, others saw cuts in services or staff, and other found they had to pay for services that were previously included or free.

Financial Structure

While many CCRCs are standalone organizations, some are part of a larger parent company, which can become worrisome for residents. For instance, if the other communities owned by the same parent company are struggling, you might be concerned that your fees are going to other facilities and not directly benefitting you.

AVOIDING THE PITFALLS

The best way to ensure that your choice of a CCRC does not include any nasty surprises is to ask questions and educate yourself. In particular, you should look into the finances of any prospective CCRC. The *Wall Street Journal* recommends that you request a copy of the facility's audited financial statements, which can give you four important pieces of information:

1. **Days of cash on hand.** You can compare this figure with other facilities, but you should expect to see about 300 days of cash on hand, give or take about twenty days. CCRCs that are part of a parent company average 281 days of cash on hand, while those with only one campus average 306 days.

2. **Cash-to-debt ratio.** This ratio should be about 35 percent, according to the *Wall Street Journal.*

3. **Information about bond financing.** The terms of such bonds typically include having 300 days of cash on hand and a minimum of 25 percent cash-to-debt ratio. Make sure your facility is meeting its lender's terms.

4. **Source of operations budget.** If a facility is relying on investment income, donations, or entry fees for its day-to-day functioning, that is a red flag. Your facility should be able to sustain itself based on income from operation.

If your CCRC does not want to provide you with this kind of information, it's time to move on to another facility.

Consumer Guide to Understanding Financial Performance and Reporting in CCRCs

The Commission on Accreditation of Rehabilitation Facilities (CARF) has put together a free guidebook of information and questions for determining the financial health of CCRCs. You can find CARF's consumer guide at *www.carf.org/financialperformanceccrcs/*.

TAX BREAKS MITIGATE THE COSTS OF CCRCS

There is no getting around the fact that retirement communities are expensive to join. However, it is possible to mitigate some of those costs, thanks to Uncle Sam. If you are joining a CCRC and are contracted for healthcare services in the future, the IRS views a portion of your nonrefundable entrance fee as a prepayment for those healthcare services, meaning you get a tax deduction on that portion. If your entrance fee is fully refundable, then you cannot claim this tax deduction. If it is partially refundable, you can claim the full deduction at the time of payment, but you or your estate may owe the IRS a portion of that tax deduction if you end up leaving or dying before the refund period has expired.

You are also entitled to a deduction for a portion of your monthly fees for a life care contract, since your payments entitle you to a lifetime of healthcare.

The deductible portion of your fees will vary from facility to facility, because each one has a different structure for payments. However, you can expect to deduct between 30 percent and 40 percent of your fees.

These deductions are also available for family members if they are providing more than half of the financial support of the CCRC resident. In either case, it's a good idea to consult with your accountant or tax preparer to make sure you are taking advantages of all the available tax breaks.

Finding the Right Fit

Just as you wouldn't choose a college to attend based solely on how nice its dorms are, you want to make sure you look at the retirement community as a whole before deciding that any one should be your new home.

The following four questions can help you zero in on particular communities that are more likely to be a good fit:

1. **What kinds of recreational programs are offered?** This question can give you quite a bit of information, starting with whether you'll find friends with similar interests. In addition, since it can be difficult to get a sense of the age of residents at a retirement community (it's always changing), a look at a typical week's activities can give you a better idea of whether the population skews more toward young retirees playing racquetball or elderly residents learning to knit.

2. **How close will you be to the "outside world"?** Many retirement communities are built wherever land is cheapest, which is often quite a distance from the nearest city or town. Living away from a larger community can lead to feelings of isolation, particularly if you don't feel engaged by the offered activities or you are far away from family or friends.

3. **What are the guest policies?** Some retirement communities have caps on the number of nights that guests (and specifically minors) can stay over. This is to discourage residents from having their underaged family permanently moving in, but such policies can make it difficult to spend time with children or grandchildren.

4. **How easy will it be for you to age in place?** While the entire point of a retirement community is to allow you to age in place, some facilities do a better job of supporting your independence than others. For instance, if you need to stop driving, does the facility have a bus or shuttle to common shopping destinations,

or will you be stuck with whatever options are available on campus? Try to imagine living in each retirement community as an elderly man or woman, and see if the place still seems appealing.

Once you have narrowed down your options, it's a good idea to try to get a sense of what life would really be like in your chosen community. To do that, make several unannounced visits at various times of the day, and take in a couple of different meals in the dining room. That will do more to give you a true feeling of the community than any tour or a brochure possibly could.

Chapter 10 Takeaways

1. There are four different types of retirement communities: 55+, Independent Living, Assisted Living, and Continuing Care (CCRC). Of these, the last is by far the most complicated, but it may also provide you the best range of options.

2. When you move into a CCRC, you will come under one of three types of contracts: Life Care, Modified, or Fee for Service.

3. If you join a CCRC, expect to pay a large fee up front for joining. This can be somewhat mitigated by tax breaks.

4. Investigate carefully what services your CCRC provides, how old the average resident is, how close the facility is to the outside world, and how easy it will be for you to age in place.

How to Retire Abroad

WHAT YOU'LL LEARN IN THIS CHAPTER

Imagine spending your golden years in an exotic, sunny locale, meeting new friends, enjoying delicious food, and living life at a happier pace. You might be surprised to learn that this romantic dream can be an economical reality for the average American retiree. In this chapter, we will discuss the dollars and cents of retiring overseas—and explore some of the issues you may face while managing your money outside of the United States. You will learn what to expect tax-wise from Uncle Sam when you call another country home. We will explore what retiring abroad will mean for Social Security, Medicare, and your citizenship. You will walk through the particulars of planning for healthcare abroad. You will learn some tips for making a foreign relocation as smooth as possible. And you will learn about five of the top Latin American retirement destinations and what makes them so attractive to American retirees.

Costs of Retiring Abroad

While retiring abroad has the potential to be expensive depending on where you move and what lifestyle choices you make there, the fact of the matter is that a flexible retiree can retire comfortably and contentedly outside of the United States for much less money than a similar retirement would cost at home. According to Suzan Haskins and Dan Prescher, the married authors of *The International Living Guide to Retiring Overseas* *on a Budget: How to Live Well on $25,000 a Year*, their living expenses in retirement in Cotacachi, Ecuador, total $1,397 per month.

What goes into such a limited budget? Haskins and Prescher assure their readers that they are not living like twenty-something backpackers, and talk freely about their splurges on everything from travel to wine to fine dining. Living expenses are simply cheaper in many foreign countries. Let's take a look at some of the costs Haskins and Prescher outline.

HOUSING

According to Haskins and Prescher, "The average rental property in the countries most popular with expatriates starts at about $300 a month. And that's for something very basic, often (but not always) unfurnished . . . Where we live, you might expect to pay $600 a month for a nice, fully furnished, two- or three-bedroom rental . . . possibly even with utilities and Internet included."

Owning your home is also an inexpensive proposition in many retiree-friendly foreign countries. You can find comfortable homes for sale in many parts of Central and South America (and even in some areas of Europe) for prices that seem ludicrously low to those used to the American housing market—$59,000 to $300,000.

UTILITIES

For the most part, utilities will cost less when you retire abroad. Some of this has to do with the lower cost of living (cell phone and Internet costs are both lower in Central and South America, for instance), although certain utilities, such as electricity, are more expensive in some areas. However, you may also save on utilities by moving to a temperate climate, like an area of higher elevation in a tropical country. Living in the Andes Mountains, for example, would mean your home is comfortable year-round without the need for heating or air conditioning.

TAXES

We'll discuss your American tax obligations later in this chapter, but you'll likely be pleasantly surprised at how low property and other taxes are in your adopted home. Haskins and Prescher note that they only pay $52 for their annual property taxes in Ecuador.

FOOD

One of the many benefits of retiring abroad is having easy access to delicious and fresh produce, seafood, and spices. In general, if you are willing to eat like a local—which often means you shop daily for fresh ingredients—then your grocery budget will be much lower living abroad. If you are committed to your favorite American brands and foods, however, you'll pay a premium for them. For instance, a can of Campbell's soup can cost as much as $4.50 in South America.

TRANSPORTATION

Unlike America, where it is nearly impossible to live outside of a major city without a car, you will probably find that you can be happily car-free in your adopted home. Public transportation tends to be inexpensive and easy to use.

It is a good idea to plan for the cost of traveling back to the United States, however, which Haskins and Prescher budget at $1,000 per round-trip plane ticket.

ENTERTAINMENT

Everything from dining out to theater tickets tends to be cheaper in Central and South America, so even your fun splurges will have less of an impact on your budget.

> ### The Expatistan Cost of Living Index
>
> You can determine the specific differences in cost of living between your current and future home with the excellent website *www.expatistan.com/cost-of-living*. This site allows you to compare the cost of your home city with 1,888 international destinations.

Handling Your Finances While Living Abroad

Thanks to modern technology, managing your finances overseas does not have to be an onerous task. You don't even need to give up your American bank account, since most routine financial transactions can be handled online. However, some advance planning and organization can help save you money and headaches.

BANKING

Many foreign retirement destinations are all about paying in cash. For these countries, you can expect to pay everyone—from your utility providers to your dentist to your grocer—in cash. That can make an expat's financial life a little simpler, as you can plan on maintaining your American bank account, provided you can withdraw funds from an ATM in your new home. As long as your American bank offers free or low-cost ATM transactions and has favorable foreign currency exchange rates, then you might feel no need to bank with a local institution in your new home. (And of course, you can always switch to another American bank with better rates and conditions before you move.)

It's important to note, however, that some countries have residency requirements for foreigners that include opening a local bank account. The government of your new home may require you to have a certain amount of money deposited in a local bank account each month, or require you to maintain a certain balance in such an account, in order to keep your residency. Your regular deposits could be direct deposits of your Social Security benefits (we'll talk more about Social Security and living abroad later in this chapter), or you could set up an automatic transfer from your investment accounts into your local bank.

Be Sure to Budget for Startup Costs

Just because the cost of living in your new home is lower does not mean you can skimp on budgeting for startup costs. In your first few months living abroad, expect to pay several one-time expenses for things such as visas, rental deposits, household goods, and the like. Haskins and Prescher recommend budgeting about $3,000 for a single expat retiree and about $6,000 for a couple.

If you are required to open a local bank account, here are several issues that you may have to consider:

- Before opening an account, find out if deposits into your new bank account are insured and the maximum amount up to which they are insured.
- You may need a resident's visa in order to open a checking account, but many banks will allow nonresidents to open a savings account.
- Opening a local account will require some additional paperwork, such as a letter of introduction from a local attorney, some local references (who can be other expats), a copy of your passport, and a local utility bill (which does not need to be in your name) for verification of your address.
- Having a foreign bank account adds additional reporting requirements to your U.S. taxes. Under the Foreign Account Tax Compliance Act, you must file a Foreign Bank and Financial Account report with the U.S. Department of the Treasury if your foreign bank account ever has a balance greater than $10,000 during a calendar year. (More on this later in the chapter.)

It Might Pay to Maintain a U.S. Address

Whether you open an account in your new home or not, entirely giving up an address in the United States could potentially cause you some administrative headaches. Provisions of the Patriot Act allow American banks to close accounts that do not have an American address associated with them. These provisions are designed to stop the financing of international terrorists, but it can be a bureaucratic nuisance for innocent expats who made a wholehearted move. Some expats have gotten around this potential problem by maintaining a mailing address (such as a P.O. box) in America.

Taxes

No matter where an American citizen hangs his hat, the IRS expects him to file taxes each year. For the most part, filing taxes while living abroad is very similar to the process at home. However, there are some specific differences and requirements that you need be aware of in order to stay on Uncle Sam's good side.

REQUIRED FEDERAL INCOME TAX FORMS

Like every taxpayer in America, expats are required to fill out a 1040 Form each year. In addition to the 1040, however, you may also need to complete Form 2555, Foreign Earned Income (*www.irs.gov/form2555*), Form 1116, Foreign Tax Credit (*www.irs.gov/form1116*), and Form 8938, Statement of Specified Foreign Financial Assets (*www.irs.gov/form8938*).

In particular, Form 8938 asks you to report financial assets that you hold outside of the United States that fall above a reporting threshold. Qualifying assets include bank accounts, brokerage accounts, mutual funds, unit trusts, and other types of financial accounts. The reporting threshold for unmarried expats is $200,000 and for married expats is $400,000.

It's important to note that this is not the only reporting require-ment for financial assets. As I mentioned previoulsy, you are also required to report foreign assets greater than $10,000 to the Department of the Treasury using Financial Crimes Enforcement Network (FinCEN) Form 114, Report of Foreign Bank and Financial Accounts (FBAR) at *http://bsaefiling.fincen.treas.gov/main.html*. Failure to file FinCEN Form 114 can result in automatic penalties of anywhere from $10,000 to 50 percent of the balance of the account, and possible criminal charges. This form must be received by the Department of the Treasury by June 30 of each year.

EXCLUSIONS, CREDITS, AND DEDUCTIONS

The good news for expats is that you are still eligible for some tax mitigation even though you no longer reside in the United States. If you earn an income, have housing expenses, or pay foreign taxes in your new home, then you may be able to reduce your federal tax burden.

Foreign Earned Income Exclusion

This exclusion is available to any U.S. citizen earning a foreign income who qualifies as a bona fide resident of another country for an uninterrupted period that includes an entire tax year.

Foreign Housing Exclusion or Deduction

You can potentially claim either an exclusion or a deduction from gross income for your housing amount if your tax home is in a foreign country and you are either a bona fide resident or spend at least 330 days in your foreign home during a period of twelve consecutive months.

Deduction of Foreign Taxes Paid

You can reduce the tax you owe the IRS on foreign income if you have already been taxed on that income in your country of residence.

FILING DETAILS

As in the United States, you are welcome to file your return electron-ically or mail it in, although there are some situations (such as when you are filing a return older than three years) when you must mail in your paperwork rather than e-file.

Citizens living abroad automatically receive a two-month extension on the general filing deadline of April 15, making the expat deadline June 15. However, any taxes owed are still due on April 15, regardless of when you finish filing the paperwork.

Finally, the IRS offers international tax assistance at their office in Philadelphia. The office is open Monday through Friday from 6:00 A.M. to 11:00 P.M. EST, and can be contacted by:

- Phone: 1 (267) 941-1000
- Fax: 1 (267) 941-1055
- Internet: (for general questions only) *www.irs.gov/uac/Help-With-Tax-Questions-International-Taxpayers*
- Mail: Internal Revenue Service, International Accounts, Philadelphia, PA 19255-0725

Citizenship and Entitlements for an American Abroad

As an American, you retain your citizenship wherever you live, unless you actively work to renounce it. In most countries, a residence visa will allow you to live indefinitely in your adopted home while maintaining your American citizenship. In some countries, you don't even need a residence visa—a tourist visa will allow you to reside there indefinitely.

Along with citizenship come many of the perks. You are still eligible to vote for candidates for federal office using an absentee ballot, and depending on where you are from, you may be eligible to vote in state and local elections in your home state. The Federal Voting Assistance Program (*www.fvap.gov*) can give you more information on how to vote as an absentee.

In addition, you can still collect Social Security benefits while living abroad, and in many cases you can have your benefits directly deposited into a foreign bank account. As mentioned previously, some countries require foreign residents to have a regular direct deposit into a local bank account, and many retired expats use their Social Security benefits to fulfill this obligation.

As for Medicare, that is one entitlement that you cannot use overseas. Medicare coverage is specific to American medical service providers. You may find better and lower-cost healthcare coverage options in your new home, but you may still wish to enroll in Medicare so that you can return to America in case of a serious medical issue. Considering the fact that there are severe financial penalties if you enroll in Medicare after your initial enrollment period (the seven months that include the three months prior to, the month of, and the three months after you turn sixty-five), think carefully about whether or not you will need Medicare before deciding to forego it.

To help you decide, let's take a look at what you can expect from healthcare outside of the United States.

Americans and Foreign Healthcare

Superior healthcare is one of the many reasons why 373,224 retired Americans have chosen to live abroad as of 2013. Not only does medical care (including insurance) tend to be much more affordable in Central and South America, Europe, and Asia, but the quality of healthcare is generally excellent, and the service—from getting an appointment to doctors' bedside manners—is much better than many Americans have come to expect from their healthcare service providers. In addition, Haskins and Prescher note that many of the doctors you'll encounter in the most popular retirement destinations have studied at some of the world's most prestigious medical schools and hospitals—which often means your doctor will speak English.

Here's what you can generally expect from enrolling in healthcare in a foreign country:

1. A Two-Tier System

Many of the countries most popular with expats offer free or very low-cost public healthcare to all citizens and legal residents. This healthcare system is subsidized by the government, and it has all of the advantages and disadvantages of socialized medicine. In addition to this, however, you will often also find private hospitals and private practice doctors whom you can pay out of pocket or purchase private medical insurance to see. Many expats mix and match the public healthcare option with some sort of private insurance.

2. Public Health Concerns

Since the public healthcare systems are set up to provide healthcare for all, you are more likely to face long wait times for appointments. In addition, you are more likely to encounter English-speaking doctors and staff in private practice—and in fact, depending on where you are, it can be unlikely that the support staff in public health clinics will speak English.

3. Coverage When You Travel

Whether you are making regular trips back to the United States or are traveling through neighboring countries, you will need to think about health insurance for when you travel. Public healthcare does not cover you outside of your country of residence, and not all private health insurance you can buy in your adopted home will take care of you if you get sick while traveling.

Expats and the Affordable Care Act

If you are younger than sixty-five when you move abroad, you may be concerned about whether you are required to carry U.S. health insurance to avoid the Affordable Care Act's penalty. There is no need to worry. American citizens living abroad for at least 330 days in a given year, or those meeting the requirements for bona fide residency in another country, are exempt from the health insurance mandate.

Making Your Transition a Smooth One

Before you start the process of retiring abroad, make sure you've thought through all of the following questions.

DO I SPEAK THE LOCAL LANGUAGE?

It's best to learn as much of the local language as possible—in advance. Taking a course at a local community college can be a good way to start preparing for your move. It's also a good idea to let go of any preconceptions you may have about how easily you will communicate in your adopted tongue, even if you are already familiar with the language. You will make embarrassing language mistakes, and having a good sense of humor about yourself will make these much easier to laugh off.

DO I KNOW WHAT THIS AREA IS LIKE YEAR ROUND?

Haskins and Prescher recommend that potential expats spend time in the new country during the worst season of the year. You may love a country's vacation weather, but you won't know that the rainy season or the mosquito season is a deal-breaker until you've lived through it.

DO I KNOW WHAT LIFE IS REALLY LIKE FOR A LOCAL?

It can be hard to remember that people all over the world live very differently than we do in America. For instance, Haskins and Prescher point out that "life is often noisier abroad." You might have crowing roosters for neighbors, or regular music festivals in the streets of your new home. Additionally, Americans are used to convenience and directness in their business matters—for everything from ordering a pizza to negotiating the price of a car—and they might be thrown off by the more laid-back attitudes they find overseas.

DO I HAVE AN EXIT STRATEGY?

A common piece of advice for potential expats is to "try before you buy." Often, renting an apartment for a few months in your adopted home while maintaining your residence in the United States can help you ease into your life as an expat. You'll learn about your new home and have the time to search for a more permanent abode. And if you find that you are homesick, it will be much easier to return to the United States.

Finding the Right Place to Call Home

While any number of countries could make for a lovely place to retire, there are several that are perennial favorites among American expats. The following five Central and South American countries offer many advantages (including relative proximity to the United States) to the expat retiree. This is not an exhaustive list, and you can find a thorough examination of these and other expat-friendly locales in *The International Living Guide to Retiring Overseas on a Budget: How to Live Well on $25,000 a Year* by Suzan Haskins and Dan Prescher.

Expat-Friendly Retirement Destinations in Central and South America

COUNTRY	WHAT MAKES IT EXPAT-FRIENDLY
Belize	English is the national language
	Low local taxes
	The Belize dollar is pegged to the U.S. dollar at 2:1
	Qualified Retired Persons Program offers benefits to retired expats
Costa Rica	The most stable democracy in Latin America
	Low local taxes and low cost of living (although real estate is relatively expensive)

	World-class healthcare at affordable prices
	A strong expat community
Ecuador	Official currency is the U.S. dollar
	Retiree benefits to residents over age sixty-five (including a law stating you never have to stand in line at the bank or utility office)
	Low local taxes and low cost of living (Haskins and Prescher live well on $1,397 per month)
	A strong expat community
Mexico	Close proximity to home
	Familiar brands and amenities are easily available
	Low local taxes and low cost of living
	High-quality healthcare and a stable economy
Panama	Official currency is the U.S. dollar
	The *Pensionado*, which is widely regarded as the best retirement program in the world, is available to expat retirees
	Low cost of living
	A strong U.S. expat community, due to our long relationship with the country

Chapter 11 Takeaways

1. Living abroad can significantly lower your expenses, depending on where you live.

2. You can often maintain an American bank account and access cash you need through ATMs.

3. You will still have to file U.S. taxes. In particular, you'll have to report financial assets held outside the United States.

4. It's a good idea to keep your American citizenship while living abroad. Among other things, this allows you to collect Social Security benefits.

5. Healthcare abroad is generally excellent and less expensive than in the United States.

CHAPTER 12

How to Travel in Retirement

WHAT YOU'LL LEARN IN THIS CHAPTER

Traveling ranks as one of the top two goals retirees have for their retirement—second only to spending time with friends and family. But although travel is a high-ranking goal for the majority of retirees, fewer than 20 percent of employees specifically save money for travel in retirement, according to a survey by the Transamerica Center for Retirement Studies. If you are among the majority of workers who dream of travel but haven't planned for it, it's not too late. This chapter will outline several strategies for affording travel in retirement, even if you have caviar tastes on a tuna budget. You will walk through what issues you need to consider if you want to follow the great American retirement plan: living footloose and fancy-free in an RV. You will understand how Medicare can work for you, and what insurance you might need to protect your health and your finances on your travels. Finally, you will learn tips for making sure you enjoy every moment of your post-retirement travel.

How to Afford Travel in Retirement

Whether or not you will be able to indulge your dreams of post-retirement travel depends entirely on two things:

1. How much you have saved for travel

2. How much you can reduce the costs of traveling

The good news is that it is possible to make your dreams of seeing the world come true, even if you have not yet started saving for your post-retirement travel. Let's look at some ways to add travel to your retirement budget, without sacrificing your regular lifestyle.

BUDGET FOR TRAVEL

As with any other budget line item, figuring out how much to save for travel in retirement requires some advance planning. Luckily, advance planning for travel is some of the most fun you can have legally (which we'll talk about in more detail later in the chapter).

For now, take the time to daydream about all of your travel goals. Knowing exactly what you want from your retirement travels will help you to determine how extravagant or thrifty your budget can be. Answer the questions in Worksheet 12-1 to get started:

Worksheet 12-1: Planning Ahead for Retirement Travel

1. Write out your travel bucket list. Where specifically do you want to go, and what do you want to experience?

2. What kind of traveler are you?

- Do you prefer being on "vacation," or do you like to immerse yourself in a new culture?
- Do you prefer several smaller trips, or one large trip each year?
- Do you prefer to travel in luxury, or are you willing to forego some creature comforts?
- Do you prefer to explore without an agenda, or do you like to have a specific itinerary for each trip?

3. Will some of your travel budget be designated for visiting far-flung children and grandchildren?

4. How many trips do you hope to take each year?

5. Of the destinations you listed in question #1, rank your three most important.

Based on your answers to the questions in Worksheet 12-1, you can start putting together a realistic estimate of your annual travel costs. You can determine the cost of specific travel opportunities using the travel budget calculator at *www.independenttraveler.com/travel-budget-calculator*. From there, you can extrapolate out how much money you will need in your annual retirement budget for travel.

Before you despair that your travel dreams are too big for your budget, keep in mind two things:

- Travel is likely not going to be a budget item forever. Most retirees do their heaviest traveling before they reach their midseventies.
- Travel has known health benefits, and it can be a good idea to view traveling in retirement as an investment in your good health and well-being.

If you long to travel but don't have room in your budget to save for it, don't forget that it is always possible to create a second income stream—no matter where you are on your path to retirement. You could always work a part-time job in your off hours, but it's good to remember that current technology has opened up worlds of income-producing activities that were not previously available. Here are some ideas for adding income without exhausting yourself with a second job:

- Freelance writing for the Internet. Sites such as Elance (*www.elance.com*) and Demand Studios (*www.create.demanstudios.com*) make it easy to start freelancing with no prior experience.
- Blogging. Making money through writing and running your own blog is not going to be easy or quick. However, many individuals

who have a passion for their blogging subject and a willingness to do the legwork to find advertisers can make a decent amount of money through blogging. If this is something you'd be interested in doing, I recommend the excellent website How I Make Money Blogging (*www.howimakemoneyblogging.com*) by professional personal finance blogger Crystal Stemberger.

- Selling crafts. The artists' marketplace Etsy (*www.etsy.com*) has made it possible for every hobby knitter, quilter, painter, and bookbinder to find a market for their wares.
- Designing and selling T-shirts. If you have a good sense of design and can craft humorous or ironic phrases and logos, you can start your own T-shirt store at sites such as CafePress (*www.cafepress.com*) and Spreadshirt (*www.spreadshirt.com*).
- Dog-sitting or dog-walking. If you love animals, offer to help your neighbors take care of their four-footed family members.
- Tutoring. If you know a subject cold, offer to tutor local high school and college students.
- Mystery shopping. Stores need mystery shoppers to check out customer service compliance. You get paid to shop at local stores and report your experience. Do be wary, however, since there are many mystery shopping scams out there. Double-check any mystery shopping offers with the Mystery Shopping Providers Association (*www.mspa-na.org*).
- Sell your photography online. If you're an amateur photographer, you can sell your pictures online as stock photography at sites like Shutterstock (*www.shutterstock.com*).

How to Reduce the Cost of Travel in Retirement

If socking money away is one side of the retirement travel coin, the other side is figuring out how to travel on the cheap. You might think that traveling on a shoestring is a young person's game and that you are too old to play it, but it's possible to travel as a retiree both comfortably and inexpensively. If you are willing to do the research, you can save money on transportation, on accommodations, and on package deals.

SAVE MONEY ON TRANSPORTATION

In general, getting to your destination will be your biggest travel expense—which means it's a prime goal to cut costs without seriously affecting your experience. Here are several ways to make sure that getting there takes a smaller bite out of your budget.

Travel Off-Season

One of the biggest advantages that traveling retirees have over ordinary tourists is that they are not tied to typical vacation schedules. This is true for everything from days of the week they are able to fly (Tuesdays and Wednesdays tend to be cheaper than weekends) to months of the year they are free to go on vacation (off-season rates are always lower than peak rates).

Don't Rely Exclusively on Online Flight Search Engines

According to professional world traveler Nora Dunn, "If you solely use the big online search engines to book your flights, there is a good chance that you are overpaying—sometimes dramatically." In addition to searching on sites such as Kayak (*www.kayak.com*) and Orbitz (*www.orbitz.com*), it pays to dig deeper. Dunn recommends the site WhichBudget (*www.whichbudget.com*), where you can search budget airlines. Another suggestion Dunn makes is to check the website of your departure or arrival airport for a list of the airlines that fly there—and then book directly with the airline. Using these strategies, Dunn has saved up to 80 percent on fares listed on the typical flight search engines.

Ask for Senior Discounts

Your AARP card can score you discounts on everything from airfare to accommodations to car rentals to tours.

Use Credit Card Miles

There is a thriving subculture of travel hackers who manage to see the world for next to nothing thanks to rewards points they have earned on their credit cards. If you are confident in your ability to hack your credit card usage without being tempted to overspend (and that is a big if!), using rewards cards could be an excellent way to reduce the cost of travel. Both NerdWallet (*www.nerdwallet.com/travel-miles-credit-cards*) and Frugal Travel Guy (*www.frugaltravelguy.com*) offer an excellent introduction to the world of earning credit card rewards points.

Make Getting There Part of the Vacation with a Repositioning Cruise

The majority of cruise lines will reposition their ships twice a year to take advantage of seasonal climates. These repositioning cruises are available for passengers at 30 to 70 percent off the regular price of cruising, with all of the onboard services and amenities that a regular cruise offers, although there are usually fewer ports of call. The only potential downside to a repositioning cruise is the fact that you will have to fly one-way from the destination city to return home. However, if you plan to stay at your cruise destination for several weeks, a repositioning cruise can be an affordable way to get there and lower your transportation costs while making travel more enjoyable. Both *www.repositioningcruise.com* and *www.cruise.com* can offer you information on repositioning cruises.

SAVE MONEY ON ACCOMMODATIONS

After airfare, the next biggest travel expense is accommodations. However, savvy travelers can stay in their favorite destinations inexpensively—or for free! Professional traveler Nora Dunn recommends several methods for reducing the cost of your stay:

1. **Travel slowly.** That is, stay in one place for a while, rather than trying to see "The Greatest Hits of Europe" in one whirlwind tour. If you only visit a few destinations, then you will be able to find cheaper accommodations (like a short-term apartment rental) that will allow you to cook for yourself, which will save

you even more money. Sites such as Airbnb (*www.airbnb.com*) and Vacation Rentals By Owner (*www.vrbo.com*) can help you find apartments, homes, and vacation rentals that will allow you to travel slowly and live like a local.

2. **Work for your accommodation.** There are countless accommodations all around the world that are willing to host travelers for free in exchange for some light work. The expectations for work-in-trade can range anywhere from doing farm work to cleaning to simple housesitting. Dunn recommends the website House Carers (*www.housecarers.com*) for travelers interested in house- and pet-sitting (which is a particularly retiree-friendly work-in-trade situation) and Help Exchange (*www.helpx.net*) for a variety of work-in-trade duties.

3. Use a hospitality exchange. Believe it or not, homeowners around the world are willing to open up their homes to guests they do not know, free of charge. Hospitality exchanges are generally for a shorter term than work-for-accommodation stays (usually no more than a week), which can work well for retirees on less ambitious trips. Since you're a houseguest, the etiquette is just what you'd expect: plan to bring a host gift and expect to help out with things such as dishes and other chores around the house. In some cases, you will be expected to also open your home up to other guests when you return, á la Cameron Diaz and Kate Winslet in *The Holiday*. Find a hospitality exchange at Couchsurfing (*www.couchsurfing.com*), Global Freeloaders (*www.globalfreeloaders.com*), which requires reciprocating hosting, or the granddaddy of hospitality exchange—Servas (*www.joomla.servas.org*), which has been around for fifty years and is recognized by the United Nations.

SAVE MONEY ON PACKAGE DEALS

Tours, cruises, and other package deals can take the headache out of travel, as well as make some destinations affordable for the average retiree. Here are several options that can help you scratch your itchy feet for less:

1. **Book cheap cruises and tours at the last minute.** It used to be that waiting until the last minute was a good way to get a low rate on every aspect of travel, from airfare to hotels. Unfortunately, modern technology has made last-minute deals on flights and hotels mostly a thing of the past—but you can still find great prices on last-minute cruises and tours, since the companies will be desperate to fill unsold spots. You can find cruise prices as low as 50 percent off if you wait to book until within a few weeks of departure. The website Cruise Sheet (*www.cruisesheet.com*) can help you find hidden deals. As for tours, look at last-minute deals offered by your preferred tour operator. For instance, Intrepid Travel (*www.intrepidtravel.com*) is a well-regarded tour company that offers last-minute deals right on its homepage.

2. **Become a road scholar.** Road Scholar (*www.roadscholar.org*) is a not-for-profit organization offering educational travel opportunities to seniors. There are 5,500 different tours to choose from in all fifty states and 150 countries, including budget-friendly tours. In addition, Road Scholar also awards $250,000 in scholarships for tours and programs in North America for interested participants of limited means.

Explore the Country in a Recreational Vehicle

Living on the open road in an RV is a common retirement dream—and one that can potentially be both economical and comfortable. The Recreation Vehicle Industry Association estimates that between 750,000 and 1 million retirees live full-time in their RVs, and the ranks are growing.

Of course, RV living isn't for everyone. If you are considering retiring to an RV, make sure you and your spouse have considered the following issues.

HOW MUCH RV DO YOU NEED?

There's a world of difference between a Class A, Class B, or Class C motor home; a fifth wheel RV, which can detach from the truck that you use to tow it; and a pop-up camping trailer. Deciding what kind of RV will work best for you depends on how far you want to travel, whether or not you want to go off-road, and how much you like your traveling companions. Make sure to match your vehicle to the types of traveling you want to do.

SHOULD YOU RENT OR BUY?

Even if you know for sure that you want to sell your house and live on the road, it's still a good idea to rent different models before you commit. If you plan to maintain your residence, you will need to use your RV regularly to make the purchase price worth it. According to The Fun Times Guide (*http://rv-roadtrips.thefuntimesguide.com*), "If you plan to use your RV the typical number of days per year (27), and you purchase [a] 3-year-old RV on credit, you will pay a premium of $200 more per day for the privilege of ownership versus renting. To make ownership financially worthwhile, you need to use your RV about 40 days per year if you buy [it] outright or about 50 days per year if you buy [it] on credit . . . For those who live full-time in their RV, the costs per day can be well under $100."

ARE YOU READY TO DOWNSIZE?

Moving from a typical suburban home to a 300-square-foot RV requires a great deal of purging. What will you do with your nonessential household goods and furniture? Can you get rid of items, or will you need a storage unit?

DO YOU KNOW HOW YOU WILL HANDLE ILL HEALTH ON THE ROAD?

We will talk in more detail about how to find doctors while away from home, but living full-time in an RV offers some unique health concerns. For instance, if you need to have a procedure or surgery, do you know where you can plan to recuperate? Will you be able to easily get prescription refills on the road?

DO YOU NEED ADDITIONAL INSURANCE?

While your existing automobile insurance policy will generally cover you behind the wheel of an RV, you ought to discuss the specifics of coverage with your insurance agent before renting or buying an RV.

ARE YOU PREPARED TO HANDLE ROUTINE MAINTENANCE?

Maintaining your RV is not exactly like maintaining your home— or your car. Do you feel comfortable handling issues that may arise, such as monitoring propane gas levels in your tanks or maintaining your generator?

Insurance Considerations

Things don't always go as planned when you travel. That's why it's crucial for you to make sure you are adequately insured before you begin your adventures in retirement. In particular, you will need to have sufficient health and travel insurance while you travel.

UNDERSTANDING THE GEOGRAPHICAL LIMITS OF MEDICARE

As we discussed in Chapter 11, Medicare coverage is specific to American medical service providers. Other than some very specific exceptions (for instance, if you get sick on a cruise ship within six hours of arrival to or departure from a U.S. port or if you need emergency medical service while traveling through Canada to Alaska), Medicare will only cover your care while you are within the United States and its territories.

However, even if you only plan to wander the width and breadth of the lower forty-eight, you still need to understand the limits of your Medicare options:

- If you have Original Medicare (which includes Part A, hospital insurance, and Part B, major medical insurance), you can receive the care you need anywhere in the United States from any doctor or hospital that accepts Medicare assignment.
- If you have a Medicare Advantage Plan (also known as Medicare Part C), you may not be covered while traveling through the United States for anything other than urgent or emergency care. That is because your plan may specify that you are not allowed to see providers outside of your network (except for emergency care), which means you will have to pay more for out-of-network care. Your Medicare Advantage Plan may also specify that you must obtain prior authorization for care, which can further limit your ability to see doctors elsewhere in the country.

If you do plan to travel abroad, it's important to note that some Medicare Supplemental Insurance policies (also known as Medigap) provide coverage for emergency care during foreign travel. Specifically, Medigap plans C through G and M and N cover 80 percent of the cost of emergency medical services during your first two months of a trip, with a $250 deductible and up to $50,000 in a lifetime. However, you cannot carry both Medicare Advantage and a Medigap policy.

THE IMPORTANCE OF TRAVEL INSURANCE

Not only can travel insurance cover your healthcare needs should you fall ill while traveling, but it can also protect you from lost luggage and canceled trips. You can purchase annual travel insurance coverage, which will take care of you no matter how often you roam during the year, or you can purchase policies for specific trips. Unfortunately, the cost of travel insurance goes up with your age, so depending on how good your health insurance is and whether you can afford to lose nonrefundable deposits and airfare should you be unable to make a planned trip, you may decide that travel insurance is more expensive than it is worth.

Get the Most Out of Your Retirement Travel

We have all experienced travel disappointment, and it can be very easy to let flight delays, minor spousal squabbles, lost luggage, or uncooperative weather make you wonder if you should have stayed home. This can be an even bigger disappointment if you have been waiting your entire life to have enough time to travel.

Experts have found that there is an excellent way to ensure that these sorts of travel disappointments do not ruin your trips: Take the time to fully anticipate your vacation.

According to psychologists who study the science of happiness, human beings feel an extra boost of pleasure if they consciously delay enjoyment. When it comes to traveling, that means that vacationers are happiest before their trips, while they are still anticipating the joys to come.

Stephanie Rosenbloom of the *New York Times* explains that there is an art to making the most of vacation anticipation. She recommends savoring your anticipation by immersing yourself in planning. For instance, you can read novels about your destination, watch films set there, listen to local music, and talk to friends who have already visited. All of these actions can induce feelings of happiness on their own—particularly chatting with friends. Adding in the anticipation of your trip will heighten your pleasure both before and during your trip.

Considering the fact that traveling during your career often leaves little time for this kind of pre-trip anticipation and immersion, it makes sense to really commit to it once you are retired and have plenty of time to make the most of your travels. Also, recognizing that anticipation can increase your enjoyment of a trip can help you to get more pleasure out of fewer trips if you are facing a limited budget.

Chapter 12 Takeaways

1. Travel in retirement is a popular goal but requires a carefully crafted savings plan.

2. Look for ways to generate additional income, as well as ways to save money on transportation and lodging during your travels (for example, by traveling in the off-season).

3. If you're thinking of traveling in an RV, consider renting before purchasing to see if you're satisfied with the experience and its costs.

4. Before beginning your travels, fully examine your insurance options, including medical and travel insurance.

5. Get the most of your trips by anticipating them.

How to Retire Early

WHAT YOU'LL LEARN IN THIS CHAPTER

Who decided that sixty-five is the perfect retirement age? Bringing your career to a close should happen when you are ready, even if it's years before the arbitrary norm. But early retirement—whether due to enthusiasm for the next chapter in your life or unforeseen circumstances that prematurely end your career—offers unique challenges and concerns. In this chapter, you will learn simple (but not easy) strategies for being able to afford an early retirement. You will explore options available to you for accessing your tax-deferred retirement income early without facing steep penalties. Last, you will walk through the most common headaches and worries plaguing a young retiree, including healthcare, inflation, and family considerations.

But let's start by tackling what seems to be the biggest stumbling block to early retirement: How do you pay for it?

Affording Early Retirement

If you listen to financial pundits, regular old retirement at age sixty-five is already out of reach for any number of workers . . . so how could it be possible for someone with an average income to retire five, ten, or even fifteen years ahead of that schedule?

It's possible if you completely change the way you look at money.

For the most part, we as Americans tend to think the answer to any money problem, including the thorny problem of retirement, is to have more money. Having a monocle-and-top-hat level of wealth is certainly one way to afford an early retirement—but it is not the only way, nor is it the best way to ensure your security and contentment.

The fact of the matter is that you really need two things in order to afford an early retirement: a large nest egg and a reduction in your spending. Learning to live well below your means while you are working can give you both, since you will not only be growing your nest egg while you are working, but you will also need less money to live on once you stop working.

So how much do you need to reduce your spending? According to the website Early Retirement Extreme (*www.earlyretirementextreme.com/ can-i-retire-young.html*), you can determine if you have cut your spending enough to afford immediate retirement with the following equation:

Your Annual Expenses < 3 Percent of Your Invested Savings

The assumption behind this equation is that the interest on your investments will cover your yearly expenses—similar to the 4 percent rule that we discussed in Chapter 5. To come up with the 3 percent number, Early Retirement Extreme is assuming that your investments will grow about 6 percent per year, while inflation will eat up about 3 percent of your growth annually.

The benefit of using this equation is that 3 percent is a very conservative projection of annual interest minus inflation, which means you can also assume that your principal will grow in the years that you earn more than 3 percent in real interest—providing you with more security.

As a matter of fact, I find the 3 percent projection to be a little too conservative. As we discussed in Chapter 5, assuming a 4 percent real return on your investment is a reasonable assumption, provided you are willing to hedge your bets with some intelligent asset allocation. (Please refer back to Chapter 5 for how to securely handle your asset allocation using the "bucket method.")

So let's take a look at some specific numbers, assuming either a 3 percent or 4 percent return:

TABLE 13-1:

Early Retirement Equation for Annual Living Expenses

RETURN RATE (ACCOUNTING FOR INFLATION)	NEST EGG	ANNUAL LIVING EXPENSES
3%	$750,000	$22,500
4%	$600,000	$24,000

Of course, any of these assumptions—that you have between $600,000 and three-quarters of a million dollars set aside and that you can live on less than $25,000 per year—can seem pretty outlandish. Who has so much money and lives on so little? No typical American does—which means those who want to retire early must embrace the atypical.

A RADICAL DEPARTURE FROM THE NORM

How little could you live on comfortably? If you're like most Americans, you might find it difficult to imagine living on much less than you make. According to a survey conducted by the Consumer Federation of America, the American Savings Education Council, and the Employee Benefit Research Institute, one-third of Americans struggle to live within their means and another one-third are able to live within their means, but have difficulty saving money. Only one-third of Americans claim to be making good progress on saving for the future. (Since they are self-reporting, that figure might need to be taken with a grain of salt, as well.)

While some of our collective inability to live below our means and set money aside for the future has to do with economic factors outside of our control—such as stagnant wages and underemployment, for instance—the fact of the matter is that many workers at every level of the income spectrum are failing to save money. That is mostly due to the consumer culture in which we live. We are constantly bombarded by messages telling us that we must own certain material items in order to be successful.

Unless you are driving a new car, living in a large house, and wearing a designer wardrobe, your success is called into question.

Those who wish to retire early must disengage from the culture of consumption. You can learn to live on much less, joyfully. Here's how one early retiree does it.

Ask the Expert: Mr. Money Mustache (MMM)

While his blogging nom de plume may be silly, MMM (who blogs at *www.mrmoneymustache.com* under that handle to protect his family's privacy) takes early retirement very seriously. He and his wife retired from traditional work at age thirty in 2005, and have been living it up with their young son on about $25,000 per year (with a $625,000 nest egg) ever since. In an interview with MarketWatch's Andrea Coombes, MMM offered several tips for reducing spending enough to be able to afford early retirement:

1. **Ride a bike.** Owning a car may not seem that expensive, but according to MMM, it can cost up to $15,000 per year in payments, maintenance, insurance, and other hidden costs. Redesigning your lifestyle to be based on walking and biking can save you that money and increase your health and happiness (and negate the need for a gym membership, to boot).

2. **How much you spend is more important than how much you earn.** This is one of the toughest lessons for people to remember, since your expenses always seem to rise with your income. You have far more control over your spending than you do over your income, and exercising that control is what will determine when you will have enough wealth to retire on.

3. **Make your money work for you.** Investing your money means that it is working for you, instead of just disappearing with each purchase. So MMM recommends keeping as many of your dollars as possible invested and working for you, rather than allowing money to just pass through your hands.

4. **Get rid of your TV.** Plugging yourself into the boob tube squanders your valuable nonwork hours and offers you negative messages about the world and the meaning of success. Without TV sucking up your time, your opportunities will start multiplying.

5. **Fill your life with riches.** Happiness is ultimately the only life goal that really makes sense. So if you work to fill your days with the things that make you happy, as opposed to the things that will impress others, then you will find you need less money than think you do.

Living on Less Is a Privilege

While I have nothing but respect for MMM's ability to live inexpensively and according to his family's values, I also recognize that his extreme retirement is a story of privilege and good fortune. For instance, very few people can afford to live within biking distance of their workplace, let alone within biking distance of two workplaces in a dual-income family.

The ability to live on very little money is dependent upon many factors that you may have little to no control over—including good health, a good education, DIY skills, and a support network. Without any one of those, an extreme early retirement will be out of reach for many people.

HOW MUCH WILL YOU REALISTICALLY NEED TO RETIRE EARLY?

Not everyone who wants to retire early is looking to hang up his or her hat at age thirty. If you want to retire in your fifties or early sixties, you do not necessarily have to follow the extreme example of MMM and other very early retirees. So what do you do if you'd like to retire ahead of schedule, but can't imagine drastically reducing your expenses or quickly building a $750,000 nest egg?

As with any retirement plan, you need to start by crunching numbers. What will your monthly expenses be in retirement? Let's revisit Worksheet 5-1: Calculating Basic Retirement Expenses from Chapter 5:

1. Calculate what your monthly expenses in retirement will be.

WORKSHEET 5-1

Calculating Basic Retirement Expenses

CATEGORY	COST
Rent/mortgage:	
Car payment:	
Groceries and household items:	
Dining out:	
Gasoline:	
Public transportation:	
Electric bill:	
Gas bill:	
Water bill:	
Trash pickup bill:	
Cable/Internet/satellite bill:	
Telephone bill:	
Cell phone bill:	
Credit card/loan payments:	
Personal care (haircuts, etc.):	
Health/dental insurance:	
Subscriptions:	
Memberships:	
Property taxes:	

Homeowners insurance:	
Car insurance:	
Miscellaneous:	
TOTAL:	

2. Multiply that number by twelve in order to determine your yearly retirement expenses:

.... ✕ 12 = ...

From here, you can use the multiplier from Table 5-2: Determining Your Expenses Multiplier to figure out how large a nest egg you will need in order to maintain your principal through your retirement:

TABLE 5-2:
Determining Your Expenses Multiplier

RETURN RATE (ACCOUNTING FOR INFLATION)	DIVIDED INTO 1	MULTIPLIER
3%	1/0.03 = 33.33	33 × Your Annual Expenses
4%	1/0.04 = 25	25 × Your Annual Expenses
5%	1/0.05 = 20	20 × Your Annual Expenses

This is another way of stating the equation from Early Retirement Extreme:

Your Annual Expenses < 3 Percent (to 4 Percent)
of Your Invested Savings

But we're not done yet.

It's important to remember that reducing your retirement expenses by a relatively small amount can drastically reduce the amount you need to retire. According to former hedge fund manager and blogger Todd Tresidder of FinancialMentor.com, "If you can figure out how to reduce your retirement budget by just $1,000 per month ($12,000 per year) . . . you just reduced how much money you need to retire by a whopping $300,000 ($12,000 × 25 = $300,000)."

So let's come up with some methods for reducing your annual expenses. Plan to implement these reductions before you retire, so that you can speed up your savings plan while also getting accustomed to living on less before the end of your career. Though this process of reducing expenses is presented to you in a single neat table, this is by no means something you can execute overnight. It can take some time to put your plans for lowering your expenses into place, so feel free to work on your action plan (your "Ways to Reduce") over the span of several weeks, or even months, if it involves major shifts (such as selling a house or a car). Even if your ways to reduce expenses are more modest, it's okay to pace yourself on the negotiations, contract changes, and other methods that require more than just a change of habit on your part. The most important thing is that you know what your expenses are and have a plan in place for reducing them.

1. Plot out methods for reducing your current and future monthly expenses:

WORKSHEET 13-2:

Reworking Your Expenses

EXPENSE	CURRENT AMOUNT	WAYS TO REDUCE	NEW AMOUNT
Rent/mortgage:			
Car payment:			
Groceries and household items:			
Dining out:			

	Current Spending		Amount Saved
Gasoline:			
Public transportation:			
Electric bill:			
Gas bill:			
Water bill:			
Trash pickup bill:			
Cable/Internet/ satellite bill:			
Telephone bill:			
Cell phone bill:			
Credit card/loan payments:			
Personal care (haircuts, etc):			
Health/dental insurance:			
Subscriptions:			
Memberships:			
Property taxes:			
Homeowners insurance:			
Car insurance:			
Miscellaneous:			
TOTALS	Current Spending $		Amount Saved $

2. Multiply the Amount Saved figure by twelve to determine your annual savings:

.... $\times$ 12 = ...

3. Calculate how the total amount saved will reduce your nest-egg needs:

.... × 25 = ...

(Assuming a 4 percent real annual return)

.... × 33 = ...

(Assuming a 3 percent real annual return)

Whatever amount you are able to shave off your annual expenses can then be invested for your retirement, bringing the end of your career that much closer. As I mentioned in Chapter 5, the formula for calculating compound interest plus your annual savings is too complicated for back-of-the-envelope math, but online calculators such as the Vanguard Retirement Income Calculator at *https://retirementplans.vanguard.com/VGApp/pe/pubeducation/calculators/RetirementIncomeCalc.jsf* can help you determine how your additional savings will increase your nest egg.

How to Access Your Retirement Income

If you are like most Americans, the money you have put aside for your retirement is in a tax-deferred vehicle such as a 401(k) or an IRA. Since there is a steep early distribution penalty of 10 percent for accessing funds from tax-deferred retirement vehicles prior to reaching age fifty-nine and a half, it may seem that early retirement would be impossible for anyone using those investment vehicles.

However, the IRS does offer some penalty-free options for early retirees who wish to access their tax-deferred accounts before they reach the age of fifty-nine and a half. In particular, early retirees will be most helped by the so-called Rule of 55 in order to access a 401(k) and by the 72(t) rule in order to access an IRA.

RULE OF 55

This is one of the simplest IRS rules out there. If you leave your employer anytime during (or after) the calendar year you reach age fifty-five, then you can access your 401(k) funds from that employer without paying the 10 percent early distribution penalty. As long as you have reached the calendar year including your fifty-fifth birthday, you are free to access that money whether you retire, are laid off, are fired, or simply quit.

There are a couple of caveats, however. If you still have money in a 401(k) plan with a former employer, you cannot withdraw money penalty-free from that plan until you reach the normal distribution age of fifty-nine and a half. If you plan to retire early, you can simply roll over any old 401(k) plans from former employers into your current 401(k) before you leave your current job at age fifty-five, since that will allow you to access all of your 401(k) funds penalty-free.

72(T) EARLY DISTRIBUTION RULE

Unlike the Rule of 55, the 72(t) Early Distribution Rule is extremely complex. The rule refers to the Internal Revenue Code (IRC) Section 72 part (t), which offers a provision for early distribution known as a Substantially Equal Periodic Payments (SEPP).

By using a SEPP, you may access funds in your IRA early and without penalty, but you must take the funds in annual (or monthly) distributions for the longer of five years or until you reach age fifty-nine and a half. (For instance, a fifty-year-old who retires and begins taking SEPP must continue the distributions until he reaches age fifty-nine and a half, while a fifty-seven-year-old retiring and accessing her IRA early must continue the SEPP until she reaches age sixty-two.)

There are three methods for determining the amount of your distribution, and all three are based upon the balance of your account and your age.

The Minimum Distribution Method

This method requires the simplest mathematical calculation of the three. You will determine the amount of your annual distribution based upon your account balance at the end of the previous year, divided by your life expectancy according to either the IRS Uniform Lifetime Table, which can be found on page 712 in Appendix A of IRS Bulletin 2002-42 (*http://www.irs.gov/pub/irs-irbs/irb02-42.pdf*), or the Single Life Expectancy Table of IRS Publication 590-B, Appendix B (*www.irs.gov/pub/irs-pdf/p590b.pdf*). In general, using the Single Life Expectancy Table will give you the most bang for your buck.

Each year, your distribution amount will be different, depending upon how much money remains in your account and the change in your life expectancy.

Example: Let's assume you are retiring in 2015 at age fifty-two, and that your IRA balance was $400,000 as of December 31, 2014. According to the Single Life Expectancy Table, your life expectancy is 32.3 years. To determine your SEPP distribution for 2015, divide $400,000 by 32.3 for an annual distribution amount of $12,384.

The Fixed Amortization Method

This method is more complex than the minimum distribution method, but it will result in an annual payment that remains the same throughout your SEPP. To calculate your distribution, you create an amortization schedule based upon your life expectancy factor from one of the two tables just mentioned, and using a rate of interest that is not more than 120 percent of the federal mid-term rate published by the IRS in an Internal Revenue Bulletin. Using this calculation, you will determine your annual distribution once and continue to withdraw the same amount each year that you are on the SEPP.

Example: The calculations required for determining an example rate are too complex to reproduce here. However, again assuming a retiring fifty-two-year-old with a $400,000 IRA balance, using the Single Life Expectancy Table, and using 120 percent of the federal mid-term rate for January, 2015, which is 2.06 percent, Bankrate's 72(t) Distribution Calculator (*www.bankrate.com/calculators/retirement/72-t-distribution-calculator.aspx*) determines an annual distribution of $17,080.

The Fixed Annuitization Method

Using this method, you will determine your annual payment by dividing your account balance by an annuity factor found on page 713 of IRS Bulletin 2002-42 (*http://www.irs.gov/pub/irs-irbs/irb02-42.pdf*), and using a rate of interest that is not more than 120 percent of the federal mid-term rate. As with the second method, once you have determined your annual distribution amount, you will continue to withdraw the same amount each year.

Example: Again, the calculations for this method are too complex to reproduce here. Using the Bankrate 72(t) Distribution Calculator and assuming the same conditions, the annual distribution using this method comes to $16,998.

While having the 72(t) Early Distribution Rule available for early retirees can be an incredible boon, it is important to note that there are some fairly big potential pitfalls. In particular, if you take too much or too little money as a disbursement, that causes the SEPP to be "busted," meaning you will pay steep penalties. All of your distributions (starting with the very first withdrawal you made) will be subject to:

- Ordinary income tax (which will have already been assessed, so no harm, no foul)
- The 10 percent non-qualified early withdrawal penalty
- Interest on any unpaid tax or penalty, calculated from the date of the disbursal up until the date that the SEPP was busted.

Considering these potential penalties, it is imperative that early retirees hoping to take advantage of the 72(t) provision work out the details with a professional who is familiar with this particular portion of the tax code.

Common Early Retirement Headaches

Retiring ahead of the typical schedule can be stressful if you are not prepared for some of the most common hazards facing young retirees. Let's take a look at some of the issues you will confront that older retirees might not have to worry about.

HEALTHCARE

If retirement income only had to cover housing, food, transportation, entertainment, and clothing, then bowing out early from a career would not necessarily be a cause for financial anxiety. But add in the high costs of healthcare, particularly during the gap between an early retirement and Medicare eligibility, and suddenly retiring ahead of the regular schedule seems out of reach. Thankfully, there are options for ensuring your health is covered.

Employer-Provided Retiree Health Benefits

If you are lucky enough to work for a company that offers health benefits to retirees, jump on it. In almost all cases, this will be your least expensive option for healthcare in early retirement, and it has the added bonus of being a familiar plan that you do not have to learn to navigate.

However, it's important to recognize that you might not be able to count on your employer's coverage throughout your retirement. First of all, many employers who offer retiree healthcare benefits have an end date of your sixty-fifth birthday, meaning that they will only cover you until you are eligible for Medicare.

What could be even more financially problematic for you is the fact that companies have no legal obligation to cover retired employees—even if they have already provided benefits to retirees. Employers may (and do) reserve the right to change the terms of their healthcare plan, which means that a retiree's benefits can potentially be cut or eliminated with no warning or recourse.

Retirees who do have health insurance benefits need to read over the Summary Plan Description (SPD) for their healthcare plan in order to determine if they could lose their benefits down the road. Unless there is specific language guaranteeing maintenance of benefits in your SPD, you may find yourself years from Medicare eligibility with no health insurance.

Your SPD will tell you if your employer promises benefits at a specified level for a specified duration. If it does not, you may be vulnerable to losing your benefits. And even if the language seems clear that your benefits are guaranteed, it is possible that your employer may change plans or benefits, triggering a new SPD—which could become the controlling document over your benefits.

The bottom line when it comes to employer-provided health benefits is that you should take advantage of them if offered, but always be aware that you could lose them with very little notice.

Individual Coverage Through the ACA's Health Insurance Marketplace

Despite a somewhat rocky launch, the Affordable Care Act (a.k.a. Obamacare) is now up and running and has helped over 15 million uninsured Americans get health insurance. Early retirees who need coverage are eligible to enroll in subsidized plans through state-based insurance exchanges.

The ACA has put limits on price variations for healthcare coverage, meaning that premiums for the most expensive coverage could not exceed 4.5 times the cost of the least expensive plan. In particular, there are only two pricing factors that insurance companies can now use to determine premium costs: age and smoking. Premium price adjustments based on age cannot exceed a ratio of 3:1, meaning a sixty-four-year-old cannot pay more than three times the amount a twenty-one-year-old would pay. (The ratio for smokers is 1.5:1). Prior to the passage of the ACA, fifty- to sixty-four-year-olds could expect to pay six to seven times what young twenty-somethings paid for individual health insurance.

In addition, the ACA guarantees coverage to any individual purchasing health insurance, despite any pre-existing conditions. The law also outlaws the practice of rescission—that is, refusal of claims to existing insurance beneficiaries based on pre-existing conditions. Also, as of 2014, annual and lifetime spending limits were eliminated for all plans offered in the Health Insurance Marketplace.

Finally, the government offers subsidies to those individuals whose income falls between 133 percent and 400 percent of the federal poverty level. These subsidies are intended to ensure that families with modest incomes do not have to pay more than a particular small percentage of their income, between 3 percent and 9.5 percent of income, toward base-level healthcare premiums. (The program assumes the base-level plan is the silver tier of health insurance plans—described in the following paragraphs—which is one step up from the least-comprehensive plans offered.)

The subsidies will be paid directly to the health insurer that the qualifying individual chooses, and will be paid in advance. In short, those who qualify for subsidies will not have to pay the entire premium themselves and then wait for reimbursement. To find out if you qualify for a subsidy through the ACA's health insurance exchange, visit Kaiser Family Foundation's subsidy calculator at *http://kff.org/interactive/subsidy-calculator/*.

Of course, premium costs are only a portion of what you need to pay for medical care. The ACA also provides financial assistance for those individuals who earn less than 250 percent of the federal poverty line ($59,625 for a family of four in 2015) for the additional costs associated with medical care—such as deductibles, copayments, and coinsurance. This aid is called cost-sharing assistance, and it was put in place to ensure that those with modest incomes can afford to go to the hospital or visit their doctor when ill.

When shopping for individual health insurance through the Health Insurance Marketplace, you will have a choice between four different "tiers" of insurance coverage. Each tier has a different actuarial value (that is, the percentage of health costs that is paid for by the insurer, rather than the patient), which affects the cost of premiums:

- Bronze: The insurer is responsible for 60% of medical costs.
- Silver: The insurer is responsible for 70% of medical costs.
- Gold: The insurer is responsible for 80% of medical costs.
- Platinum: The insurer is responsible for 90% of medical costs.

The lower the actuarial value of the insurance, the lower the premiums will be. However, there will be higher out-of-pocket costs for any healthcare received through a plan that has a low actuarial value. Nevertheless, even the lowest-cost plans in the bronze tier will have to confirm to the following minimum benefits required by the law:

1. Ambulatory patient services

2. Emergency services

3. Hospitalization

4. Maternity and newborn care

5. Mental health and substance use disorder services, including behavioral health treatment

6. Prescription drugs

7. Rehabilitative and habilitative services and devices

8. Laboratory services

9. Preventive and wellness services and chronic disease management

10. Pediatric services, including oral and vision care

Since all plans in the Health Insurance Marketplace will adhere to these minimum benefits and these tier levels, it will be easier for you to compare apples to apples in determining which plan will work best for you.

Cost-Sharing Assistance Through the ACA

Individuals and families at or below 250 percent of the federal poverty level will also be eligible for cost-sharing assistance at the silver level. Those with more modest incomes will have the actuarial value of coverage increased so that they do not have to pay the full remaining 30 percent of the cost of services that are covered by insurance. It will be as if those with incomes at or below 250 percent of poverty were enrolled in a plan with a higher actuarial value.

HANDLING INFLATION IN RETIREMENT

Inflation is a problem for any retiree on a fixed income, but young retirees are even more vulnerable. That's because it takes less time than you might think for inflation to double prices. For instance, an inflation rate of 3 percent causes prices to double in twenty-four years—which can seriously put a kink in an early retiree's financial plans.

So how do you fight inflation if you plan to be retired longer than the typical twenty-five to thirty years? It all comes down to making smart choices in both your spending and your investments.

Keep Your Personal Rate of Inflation Low

The government uses several measurements for determining the level of inflation, the most famous of which is the Bureau of Labor Statistics Consumer Price Index (CPI). This measure looks at the average change in price for a certain "basket" of eight goods and services: food, housing, apparel, transportation, medical care, recreation, education, and other. To determine the CPI, the costs of each service are weighted based upon the amount of income a typical consumer spends on each area.

What this means for you is that an overall inflation rate of 3 percent might not reflect your experience in retirement. For one thing, you are not necessarily an average consumer anymore. You may no longer have need for housing, apparel, or education expenses once your career has ended, and you might be able to lower other "average" expenses (such as transportation) by retiring.

In addition, choosing to live a thrifty lifestyle in retirement means that you get to decide when and on what you will spend your money. For instance, if the cost of beef goes up, a frugal retiree might eat more vegetarian or chicken dishes, thereby keeping her grocery bill the same despite inflation in the food sector.

As we discussed at the beginning of the chapter, you ultimately have control over your spending, which means inflation does not necessarily have to hurt your bottom line.

However, there are some spending categories, such as healthcare, where we have much less control over our purchases. To avoid depleting your nest egg because of inflation in these areas, it's important to make sure you invest with inflation in mind.

TIPS: Inflation Protected Investments

There are several ways to invest your money to protect yourself from the effect of inflation. In particular, I find using the bucket method of asset allocation (as described in detail in Chapter 5) to be one of the savviest methods of growing your wealth even while retired—which will naturally insulate you from inflation.

However, for those with lower risk tolerance, Treasury Inflation Protected Securities (TIPS) offer a safe investment with government guaranteed inflation protection. Here's how they work.

Like other Treasury bonds, TIPS pay a fixed rate of return on your investment. For instance, if you purchase $1,000 in TIPS bonds with a 2 percent rate of return, you will receive $20 per year (2 percent of $1,000) until the maturity date, at which point you receive the face value back.

However, the face value of a TIPS bond increases with the rate of inflation—as does the value of the return rate. So if inflation rises to 5 percent in the first year after you purchase $1,000 in TIPS bonds, the face value increases to $1,050, and you are paid 2 percent of that value, or $21. When your TIPS bonds mature, you are paid the face value or the original value, whichever is greater. (This means you are also protected from deflation.) TIPS are sold in increments of $100, and are issued in terms of five, ten, and thirty years.

It's important to note, however, that since TIPS are safe investments, they are also fairly low-yield investments. As of this writing, thirty-year TIPS offer interest rates of less than 0.75 percent, and the yields on five- and ten-year TIPS are even lower.

FAMILY CONSIDERATIONS

Early retirement increases the likelihood that you will have family members relying on you—either children who are not yet financially independent, or older parents who are struggling with their own retirement finances.

If you have financially dependent family, you have two choices available when it comes to getting out of the rat race early: Either save enough money so that you can continue to help out your family, or set some strict boundaries regarding what you will and will not pay for.

Neither of these options feel great. Saving more might require you to work past your retirement goal date, and setting financial boundaries with the people you love can be its own form of torture. However, as unpleasant as it might be to deal with these issues, it is far better to take the time to think through how you will handle dependent family ahead of time than find you have run out of money after you have been retired for several years.

Chapter 13 Takeaways

1. To retire early, you need a large nest egg and to reduce your spending. To retire, your annual expenses should be less than 4 percent of your invested savings.

2. To retire early you must disengage from the culture of consumption.

3. You have more control over how much you spend than how much you earn.

4. Learn the rules about accessing your retirement funds, especially your 401(k) and any IRAs.

5. Among the challenges for early retirees are healthcare costs, inflation, and family members relying on you for financial support.

CHAPTER 14

How to Change Careers in Retirement

WHAT YOU'LL LEARN IN THIS CHAPTER

Retiring from your primary career does not necessarily mean retiring from work altogether. For many retirees, leaving one career just paves the way for starting a fulfilling second career. In this chapter, you will learn how to prepare for an encore career, whether that means working for a new employer or striking out on your own as an entrepreneur. We will start by exploring the decision-making process for determining what your second career will be, as well as strategies for making the transition as smooth as possible. You will then take a look at the common mistakes career changers make, and how you can avoid them. Finally, we will discuss how your employment in retirement can affect your Social Security benefits and your retirement accounts.

Figuring Out Your Second Act

The reasons for changing careers in retirement are as varied as retirees themselves. Perhaps you shelved a career dream years ago in order to support your family, and look forward to a post-retirement job change as the opportunity to revisit that old passion. Maybe you need to eke out your nest egg, but cannot bear to think of staying indefinitely in your current career. Or maybe you are just ready for a big change, but not interested in living the typical retiree lifestyle.

No matter what is motivating you to seek a new career in retirement, it's important for you to manage your expectations for your second career. There is less leeway for a do-over when you start a new career in your fifties, sixties, or seventies. So before you leap into a new opportunity, make sure you know the answers to the following questions:

1. **Name the three most important things you hope to get from your post-career work.** It's easy to pin hopes for happiness on a new situation. But a new job cannot give you overall life fulfillment. In general, narrowing down your work must-haves to three goals is reasonable, so take the time to identify which three are most important to you from the beginning.

2. **What kind of preparation will you need to do?** If your new career requires education, licensing, or securing financing for a new business, plan on taking your time to get it lined up. Career and retirement expert Kerry Hannon suggests that the longer time frame you have to plan, the better, since it will give you plenty of time to recover from setbacks. How long a time frame? Hannon suggests taking about three years to get your ducks in a row.

3. **How can you gain experience in your new field before you make the transition?** Volunteering, moonlighting, or job shadowing are all excellent ways to dip your toe into the new work experience without fully committing to the job. Not only will these opportunities make you a more attractive and experienced candidate in your new field, but they will also give you an insider's view into the career. The job you think you want might not be as exciting or challenging as you believe.

4. **How much financial cushion do you have?** Whether you are starting at the bottom in a new company or launching your own business, it's likely that your take-home pay will be lower for

the first few years after you have made the career transition. Can you live on your reduced paycheck, or will you need to tap your retirement accounts to make up the difference? If you are going the entrepreneur route, where will your startup capital come from? (Hint: Startup capital should *never* come from your retirement accounts.)

The Retiree-Entrepreneur

Many retirees decide to become self-employed for their second career, and it can be a very satisfying career change. If you are interested in exploring your options as an entrepreneur, AARP offers a number of resources at *www.aarp.org/work/on-the-job/info-08-2012/ become-an-encore-entrepreneur.html.*

---

5. **How does your current career relate to your encore career?** No matter how different your two careers might appear, you have certainly learned skills in your first career that will be applicable in your second. Taking the time to identify the skills that you will continue to use will not only help you to prepare for your new career, but you will also be able to sell your abilities to hiring managers and lenders when you are ready for the transition.

6. **What is your exit strategy?** Do you plan to keep working at the same level indefinitely, or are you looking forward to a time when you can slow down or fully retire? What will you do if your energy starts flagging earlier than you anticipated? If you are building a business in retirement, do you have plans for keeping it running without you? Having a plan for the end of your second career—both under ideal and less-than-ideal circumstances—will help you to make the best choices throughout your encore career.

PLANNING FOR A SMOOTH TRANSITION

You will face numerous unexpected hurdles on your path to an encore career, but planning ahead can ensure that your second career isn't derailed before it gets started. To make your transition as smooth as possible, make sure you have strategies in place for dealing with everything from timing to finances to the emotional component of making a big change.

1. *Set up your SMART goals.* Many first career paths follow a meandering route, but retirees don't have the time to fall into a career that they love. They need to be deliberate and strategic—which means creating SMART goals.

   SMART is an acronym for Specific, Measurable, Achievable, Relevant, and Timely. If you have a SMART goal, you know exactly what success in achieving your goal will look like (specific), you will know when you are making progress even if it takes time (measurable), you have chosen a goal that is something you can personally do (achievable), your goal matters in your life (relevant), and you have a target date for achieving your goal (timely).

   Using SMART goals can make the difference between saying "I'd love to open a bed and breakfast someday" and actually doing it.

2. *Seek out a mentor in your new field.* In general, people love being asked for their advice. Finding a mentor in the field you are adopting can help you to figure out the essentials without trial and error.

3. *Make sure you are financially fit.* Carrying debt into your retirement is a no-no for a good reason, but retirees planning on working after the end of their primary career might believe the rule doesn't apply to them. Nothing could be further from the truth. If you are entering into a retirement career with credit card, auto loan, or mortgage debt, then you will not have the ability to pursue satisfying but lower-paying work, or have the time to allow

a post-retirement business to get off the ground. Planning to bring in a paycheck in retirement does not negate the need to get your finances completely in order.

4. *Transition slowly.* There are a number of reasons why you should make your transition a slow one:

- Taking your time will provide you with plenty of time to dot every *i* and cross every *t* without feeling exhausted or overwhelmed. If you handle a single second-career-related task at a time (such as taking a night class or pursuing the licenses you will need), you can make forward progress while still employed full-time in your first career.
- A slow transition allows you to network more effectively, as you will have plenty time to simply chat with people about your plans. You never know where an important connection will come from, and having several years to prepare for a career change will give you the time to explore your network—without getting the wild-eyed, desperate look that comes into the eyes of last-minute networkers.
- Starting over in a new career where you know very little can seriously hurt your confidence, particularly if your first day of work in your current career is decades behind you. Taking a couple of years to prepare can give you the time to build up your confidence, and you can avoid feeling incompetent as you struggle with the new path.

Common Career-Change Mistakes

While it's inevitable that you will make (and learn from) mistakes as you end one career and start another, there are some mistakes that commonly trip up retirees in your position. Make sure you don't fall victim to the following avoidable pitfalls.

DATING YOURSELF

Older job seekers often wonder if they should dye their hair in order to appear more youthful at job interviews. Instead of hiding your gray, start with your online presence, which is much more likely to mark you as outdated. Are you on social media, and particularly LinkedIn? If you do have a social media presence, are you active? Job seekers without active online connections can seem like hopeless fuddy-duddies. This doesn't necessarily mean you have to be on Twitter 24/7, but you do need to have an up-to-date profile on LinkedIn (and any other social media you use), including a recent photograph. Nothing screams "I don't really do social media" like a missing avatar photo.

In addition, you may not realize that certain e-mail addresses have lost their cachet. Individuals searching for jobs using their AOL or Yahoo e-mail accounts can seem stuck in the nineties. Gmail and Outlook are considered the modern professional options. (Full disclosure: I still use Yahoo e-mail, and although my choice does seem to amuse some of my colleagues, I have not lost any opportunities because of it.)

OVERSATURATING YOUR RESUME

You might be tempted to outline your entire work history in your resume, but that is a surefire way to lose a hiring manager's interest. Instead, you need to tailor your resume to each job that you are interested in. That way, you can highlight the specific experiences that indicate you have the skills they are looking for.

Tailoring your resume also ensures that you do not fall victim to the scattershot approach to job searches. No one has ever gotten a great job by throwing resumes at every posted opportunity—but in the new millennium, hiring managers expect good candidates to truly understand the job posting and have a resume to reflect that.

FEARING AGE DISCRIMINATION

Officially, companies cannot decline to hire you simply because of your age—but the reality is that age discrimination does exist, and it's extraordinarily difficult to root out of the hiring process. However, older job applicants need to be sure they don't focus on their fear of age discrimination, or else it may become a self-fulfilling prophecy. To combat this, make sure you remember everything that you bring to the table that no whippersnapper could possibly offer. In addition, looking the part of a confident and vibrant candidate, from your well-chosen suit to your perfect posture, can send the signal that you are ready for the job at hand.

Social Security and Your Second Career

If you decide to apply for your Social Security benefits before reaching your full retirement age, the income from your second career can negatively affect your benefits. In particular, if you are working and you start drawing benefits before you reach your full retirement age, then you will see $1 deducted from your benefits for every $2 you earn over $15,720 (as of 2015).

What is possibly a bigger issue is the fact that Social Security does not prorate these deductions. Beneficiaries who make over the income limit will find their benefits completely withheld until they have reached the full benefit reduction amount.

If you begin drawing benefits during the same year that you reach full retirement age, the income limit is higher ($41,880 for 2015) and the amount your benefits are reduced is lower—$1 for every $3 you earn above that amount. The very month that you reach your full retirement age, you will be allowed to keep every penny of your benefits, no matter how much money you are earning through other work.

However, even if your benefits are reduced in such a way, the benefit money is not gone forever. Social Security will increase your benefits once you reach your full retirement age in order to take into account the months that you had your benefits withheld.

The effect of working income on your early Social Security benefits is yet another reason why it's truly in your best interest to hold off on applying for benefits until you have reached your full retirement age.

Taxes on Your Social Security Benefits

As we discussed in Chapter 6, you may owe taxes on your Social Security benefits if your retirement income is above a base amount (between $25,000 and $34,000 for single filers, and between $32,000 and $44,000 for married couples). If you take your Social Security benefits at the same time that you are working in retirement, it is very likely that you will earn more than the base amount and will owe taxes on your benefit checks. Please refer back to Tables 6-1 and 6-2 and Worksheet 6-3 to determine what effect your second-career income could have on your Social Security benefits.

Handling Retirement Accounts During Your Second Career

One of the best perks of exploring a second career in retirement is extending the time you have to set money aside in tax-advantaged accounts. In 2015, anyone over age fifty can contribute up to $6,500 to an IRA and up to $24,000 to a 401(k) (versus $5,500 and $18,000 respectively for younger savers). In addition, if your spouse is no longer working, you can contribute up to $6,500 to his or her IRA as well, provided your earnings cover the amount of the contribution.

However, there is an end date for IRA contributions: once you reach the age of seventy and a half. At that point, you must stop contributing to your IRA and you must begin taking your required minimum distributions (RMD), or you face a stiff penalty: The IRS will take 50 percent of the amount that should have been withdrawn.

On the other hand, as long as you are working, you do not have to take an RMD from your 401(k), even if you reach the age seventy and a half. But if you still hold 401(k) accounts from previous employers, you will have to take RMDs from them. You can avoid this by rolling over older 401(k) plans into your current employer's plan.

Chapter 14 Takeaways

1. The more carefully you plan your second career, the better will be its chances of success.

2. Be confident in your age and appearance while being attuned and up to date with the culture of the career you've chosen.

3. A second career can negatively impact your Social Security benefits. It's best to hold off applying for benefits until you've reached your full retirement age.

CHAPTER 15

How to Go Back to School in Retirement

WHAT YOU'LL LEARN IN THIS CHAPTER

Going back to school after you retire is an excellent opportunity to expand your horizons, challenge yourself, and finally take those fascinating classes you couldn't fit into your life way back when. But going back to school after the end of your career—whether you are planning on seeking a degree or simply taking a class or two—can seem financially daunting. In this chapter, we will discuss the various methods retirees can use to pay for their late-in-life higher education. You will learn the myriad reasons why a 529 education savings plan can be a valuable financial tool for education in retirement. You will take a look at other financial aid available to senior scholars, including tuition assistance and tax credits. Finally, you will explore the options available for free online education.

But let's start with the surprising benefits a 529 plan can offer an older student.

Start Saving in a 529 Plan Before You Retire

You may already be familiar with the 529 plan—the tax-deferred savings account designed to help students pay for college. You may have either set one up or contributed to one for your own children or grandchildren.

What you may not know is that you can also take advantage of 529 plans for your own post-retirement education.

Here's how it works: A donor sets up the 529 account for use by a beneficiary—and the donor and beneficiary can be the same person. Once you have set up your 529, you can begin making contributions—and taking advantage of several tax benefits.

For instance, like your 401(k) or IRA, a 529 account offers tax-deferred growth, meaning your education nest egg can grow more quickly. (Unlike your tax-deferred retirement accounts, however, your contributions to your 529 are not federally tax-deductible, although if you live in one of thirty-four states offering full or partial state tax deductibility, you may still find that contributions to your 529 ease your tax burden.) In addition, as long as you use your 529 funds for qualified education expenses, your withdrawals are federal tax-free.

Which Education Expenses Are Qualified?

Qualified educational expenses include tuition, fees, books, supplies, and equipment at any accredited college, university, or vocational school in the United States. In addition, room and board can be considered a qualified expense, as long as it falls within the cost listed by the university as part of its "cost of attendance." Finally, special-needs students will find that their additional expenses necessary for enrollment will also be considered qualified.

Unqualified costs include activity fees and insurance that are not required as a condition of enrollment, a computer, transportation costs, and repayment of student loans.

You might be wondering why you would bother with a 529 account when you can make similar contributions to your IRA or 401(k), with the added bonus of federal tax-deductibility. There are a few reasons to choose a 529 plan to save for a post-retirement education rather than your traditional retirement account.

DIVERSIFY YOUR FEDERAL TAXES

While contributions to your 529 plan are not tax-deductible (in other words, you must fund the account with money that has already been taxed), the fact that qualified education expenses are free of federal tax can help you to diversify your tax burden in retirement. If you expect to have a robust retirement income—and therefore a potentially high tax burden in retirement—knowing that your education expenses will not add to your tax burden can be a boon.

It is important to note that having a Roth IRA or a Roth 401(k) will give you the same diversification of taxes. However, 529 plans do offer other incentives that make them a smart choice for any worker who is absolutely certain that she will be attending school in retirement:

- **State tax incentives.** Every state in the union offers a 529 plan, and most states will allow the plan to be transferred for use in another state, should you decide to relocate in retirement. Each state offers various tax incentives to residents for using a 529 plan within the state. The incentives vary from state to state, but in general, you will see the largest tax incentives for creating and using a 529 plan within your state of residence, and by attending a public school within your state. While these incentives do vary, they can offer you savings that you would not see should you decide to use your traditional retirement accounts for education expenses in retirement.

- **No age penalties.** 529 plans also offer retirees more flexibility than retirement accounts. If you decide to retire and begin attending school prior to reaching age fifty-nine and a half, you can access your 529 funds penalty- and tax-free (provided you are using the funds for qualified education expenses). While withdrawing funds from your IRA or 401(k) for education expenses will not be subject to the 10 percent early withdrawal penalty, you will still owe income tax on your distribution.

  In addition, retirement accounts also have required minimum distributions once you reach age seventy and a half. If you are planning to wait to go back to school until you are well into your seventies, the government will still require you to take your minimum distribution from your IRA or 401(k) at age seventy and a half, even if you are not yet ready to start your education

- **Transferability.** Should you change your mind about going to college, all is not lost. While you are able to access your 529 funds for non-qualified expenses, you will owe a 10 percent penalty and income tax on your withdrawal, similar to early withdrawals for retirement accounts.

    If you do not need to access the funds, then you can simply change the beneficiary from yourself to another family member. 529 plans allow you to change beneficiaries as often as once a year, and you can even pass your account along to future generations. All you need is the Social Security number of your potential beneficiary (so no transferring to a grandchild still in utero).

- **Estate planning.** Assets in a 529 plan are not counted as part of the donor's estate for estate tax purposes. This means that a donor can place money outside of his estate by funding a 529 plan, but he can still retain some control over that money in case he needs to access it. This rule is only for donors of 529 plans, not beneficiaries, which means you would have to name a beneficiary other than yourself in order to take advantage of this rule.

Options If You Didn't Save for Your Education

Planning ahead for the college education you hope to get in retirement is wonderful—but many people don't even realize they have a yen for higher learning until after they have been retired for a couple of years. Luckily, there are several opportunities available for making college courses affordable for retirees.

TUITION ASSISTANCE

If you are simply interested in a subject and want to learn more, many community colleges and even some four-year colleges will allow seniors to audit classes for free. This is a great opportunity for the scholar on a fixed income, although you will still have to buy your textbooks and potentially pay any class fees.

If you would like to take the class for credit, many schools will offer significantly reduced tuition for seniors, provided you are a state resident and meet age thresholds—generally sixty, sixty-two, or sixty-five and older, depending on the state. You may also have to meet income limits in order to qualify.

In addition, twenty-one states and Washington, D.C., offer statewide tuition waivers at public colleges for senior citizens. Unfortunately, there are limits on where you can use the free tuition. For instance, it may only be applicable at certain public schools or only at community colleges.

Finally, if you are over the age of fifty-five and are a regular volunteer, you may be eligible for an education award through the Edward M. Kennedy Serve America Act. These awards are available for up to $1,000 for 350 hours of volunteer service. The volunteer can use the award for him- or herself, or transfer it to a child or grandchild. You can learn more about the award at *www.nationalservice.gov/about/legislation/edward-m-kennedy-serve-america-act*.

TAX CREDITS AND INCENTIVES

Uncle Sam is happy to help you continue your education and offers several tax credits and incentives for education. But you need to remember that "double-dipping" (e.g., taking more than one tax break for the same expense) is prohibited.

The American Opportunity Tax Credit (AOTC)

This popular tax credit is currently slated to last until December 2017. With this credit, you offset your taxes by up to $2,500 per student per year, for up to four years of undergraduate education for any student enrolled at least half-time in a degree-granting program. You can use the AOTC on tuition, books, supplies, equipment, and enrollment fees.

This program is only available to students who have not already completed four years of postsecondary education. Up to 40 percent (or $1,000) of the credit is considered "refundable," meaning the IRS cuts you a check for that amount if you owe no taxes. To be eligible, single filers must earn less than $90,000 per year, and married couples filing jointly must earn less than $180,000.

The Lifetime Learning Credit (LLC)

Unlike the AOTC, this credit is available for any student to further his education, whether or not he already holds a degree. There is also no limit on the number of years you can claim the LLC, and you do not have to be pursuing a degree to be eligible. In fact, you can use the LLC for as little as one course per year. The credit is only good for tuition and fees—you're on your own for books, equipment, and supplies.

This program offers filers a 20 percent credit on education expenses (up to a $2,000 limit for the first $10,000 spent on education expenses). The LLC is not refundable. The credit is available for single filers making $62,000 per year or less, and married filers making $124,000 or less.

Tuition and Fees Deduction

This deduction will allow you to lower your taxable income by up to $4,000 per year. This program is different from both the AOTC and the LLC in that it is a deduction rather than a credit. Credits reduce your tax bill dollar for dollar; for example, your tax bill will be reduced by $2,500 with the AOTC if you qualify for the full amount. Deductions, on the other hand, reduce the amount of taxable income that you claim on your return.

You can take this deduction if you are a single filer earning $80,000 or less, or a married couple filing jointly earning $160,000 or less. (Married couples filing separately cannot take this credit.) The only qualified education expenses for this credit are tuition and fees—hence the name.

Free Education Online

Since we live in the age of the Internet, you can receive a first-rate online education for free, and in the comfort of your own home. In particular, there are two educational sites that offer outstanding instruction without costing a penny:

- **Coursera.** This is an educational program that partners with big-name universities and organizations from around the world in order to offer online courses for anyone to take. There are currently 941 different courses available through Coursera, taught by major names in a variety of fields. These courses are designed to help students master the material, and each one offers online lectures, interactive exercises, and tests of your knowledge. You can learn more at *www.coursera.org*.
- **Khan Academy.** Khan Academy also offers free education to anyone interested in learning. Their mission is to offer a free, world-class education for anyone, anywhere, which means all of their resources (which include videos, interactive content, and assessments) are completely free—forever. Khan Academy has also been fully translated into Spanish, Portuguese, and French. Learn more at *www.khanacademy.org*.

Chapter 15 Takeaways

1. If you want to go back to school in retirement, you should open a 529 account, a tax-deferred savings plan to pay for college.

2. Advantages of 529 plans include state tax incentives, no age penalties, and ease of use in estate planning. You can also change the beneficiary from yourself to someone else.

3. Look into tuition assistance or auditing classes for free. As well, you may qualify for an education award.

4. There are a number of tax incentives that support retirees who want to go back to school.

5. Free online courses are available to those interested in extending their learning.

CHAPTER 16

How to Work Part-Time in Retirement

WHAT YOU'LL LEARN IN THIS CHAPTER

Just because you are ready to retire from the nine-to-five grind does not mean that you want to give up work altogether. After all, working seniors enjoy improved physical and mental health as compared to those who retire completely, according to a study published by the American Psychological Association in 2009. The benefits of part-time work in retirement are greatest in seniors doing work that they enjoy and that allows them to make use of their strengths. In this chapter, we will discuss how to find those enjoyable part-time jobs that fit within the retirement lifestyle you want to lead. In addition, you will learn where to look for part-time jobs that offer health insurance benefits. You will also take a look at the potential pitfalls of part-time work in retirement, and how to avoid them.

Finding Enjoyable Part-Time Work

There is a reason why it's a retirement cliché to work as a Walmart greeter: It's a readily available job that does not overtax retirees. But for most seniors, it's also a mind-numbing way to supplement an income. There are much more enjoyable and stimulating ways to work part-time after you retire. The trick is to match your lifestyle and interests to your job search—and to begin thinking about your ideal part-time work before you have left your career. To start, take the time to think through exactly what you want to get from your part-time work. Make sure you know the answers to the following questions:

- How much money do you need to bring in?
- What does part-time mean to you? How many hours are you willing or able to work?
- Do you want to work regular hours every week, or would you prefer to have a seasonal job and take the rest of the year off?
- Do you have the discipline or desire to work from home? Or is getting yourself out of the house part of the draw of part-time work?
- Do you enjoy working with people?

Answering these questions can help you narrow down which kind of work will best fit within your retirement lifestyle. From there, you can begin to consider three different retirement options that can give you the mental challenge you need while allowing you more time to enjoy your life outside of work:

- *Work part-time for your current employer.* If you like what you do but would like to do less of it, downshifting to a part-time or seasonal schedule could be the best of both worlds. There are some potential pitfalls to downshifting in this way, which we will cover later in this chapter.
- *Freelance.* Continuing to work in your same field, but now as your own boss, can be an excellent way to generate income and stay sharp without overscheduling yourself. If you are unsure of how to find clients, there are a number of resources available that connect seniors to project or freelance work. Check out *www.retirementjobs.com* and *www.retiredbrains.com.*
- *Look for opportunities in the places you frequent anyway.* This tip comes from Philip Taylor, finance blogger at PTMoney.com. He suggests combining your favorite hobbies with part-time employment: "If you love to golf, look for part-time positions at your local golf

course. Similarly, you could work for a cruise line if you'd love to travel in retirement, referee for the local sports clubs if you'd be watching games anyway, or work for a college if you'd like to take classes."

Unusual Jobs for Traveling Retirees

If you plan to make the road your home, you can still find part-time work without having to settle down. The Workamper News (*www.workamper.com*) connects RVers with seasonal and part-time employers, while Coolworks.com (*www.coolworks.com/older-bolder*) offers information on seasonal and temporary employment at national parks, lodges, ranches, and other outdoor destinations.

Part-Time Jobs with Benefits

As we've discussed, healthcare costs in retirement can be exorbitant, particularly if you retire prior to reaching Medicare eligibility at age sixty-five. If you want to keep employer-sponsored healthcare, it may seem as though you have no choice but to work full-time. Thankfully, there are several major companies that offer health insurance and other benefits to their part-time employees:

Job Fulfillment and Healthcare

To go from discussing ways to find fulfilling work in retirement to list-ing retail and temporary employers that offer healthcare benefits may seem like a bait and switch. After all, working retail and temp jobs is not traditionally considered fulfilling work. However, the majority of employers who offer benefits to part-time workers are also committed to putting their employees first—so you may find that getting medi-cal insurance through your part-time employer and getting fulfillment from your days at work are not mutually exclusive goals.

---

1. **Aerotek**—This national temp agency offers generous medical benefits to its contracted workers who put in at least twenty hours per week. Medical benefits include dental and vision cov-erage, and spouses and dependent children under the age of twenty-six are also eligible for the insurance. For a retiree who needs health coverage for other family members, this would be an excellent employer to join. (*www.aerotek.com*)

2. **Chico's FAS**—Chico's FAS is the umbrella under which you'll find four clothing retailers: Chico's, White House | Black Market, Soma Intimates, and Boston Proper. If you become a part-time associate at any of these stores, you will be eligible to purchase limited medical, dental, and vision coverage through your employer. (*http://jobs.chicos.com*)

3. **The Container Store**—This organization superstore has been on *Fortune*'s 100 Best Companies to Work For list for fifteen years in a row, and for good reason. Part-time employees are eligi-ble for medical, dental, and vision coverage, as well as a 401(k) plan with discretionary employer match, pet insurance, term life insurance, paid time off, and discounts on gym memberships. (*www.containerstore.com/careers/index.html*)

4. **Cost Plus World Market**—This specialty retail store stocks furniture, décor, wine, craft beer, and international food products. Part-timers are eligible for a limited benefits plan geared toward preventive care and wellness. (*www.worldmarketcorp.com/careers*)

5. **Costco**—Part-time Costco employees who average twenty hours per week are eligible for the health benefit plan, as well as a basic dental care plan, after 180 days of employment. In addition, most Costco stores have both pharmacies and vision centers, which means employees can use their vision care and drug benefits right at work—and copays on generic drugs can be as low as $5. (*www.costco.com/jobs.html*)

6. **Fifth Third Bank**—The banking giant offers fairly generous benefits to part-time employees who put in more than twenty hours per week. These benefits include health, dental, vision, and life insurance, all available to employees after an initial thirty-day waiting period. (*www.53.com/careers/index.html*)

7. **Lowe's**—The home improvement giant gives its part-time employees access to health, vision, dental, disability, and life insurance plans as of the date of hire. The health plan is a limited care plan, so it may not cover all the medical needs you may have. However, Lowe's also provides vacation accrual for part-timers, as well as a 401(k). (*http://careers.lowes.com*)

8. **REI**—This outdoor gear retailer provides benefits for employees who work a minimum of twenty hours a week. These benefits include a part-time health plan, for which REI pays the majority of the costs, as well as basic life and disability insurance. Employees may also purchase additional coverage like vision care, orthodontia, and long-term care insurance. (*http://rei.jobs*)

9. Starbucks—Becoming a part-time barista at one of the over 21,000 Starbucks locations in the world will not only score you a free pound of coffee per week, but it will also provide you with medical, dental, life, and disability insurance. Employees only need to work 240 hours quarterly (just about twenty hours per week) to be eligible. (*www.starbucks.com/careers/ working-at-starbucks*)

Potential Part-Time Pitfalls

Working part-time may seem like the perfect way to supplement your retirement income and keep yourself busy. But there are some potential downsides to this retirement plan, which might actually put a crimp in your budget. Here are the issues you need to be wary of before taking that part-time position.

SOCIAL SECURITY INCOME

As we discussed in Chapter 14, if you are receiving Social Security benefits while you are working, you will see $1 deducted from your benefits for every $2 you earn over $15,720 (as of 2015). If you wait to begin drawing benefits until the year you reach full retirement age, the income limit is higher ($41,880 for 2015) and the amount your benefits are reduced is lower—$1 for every $3 you earn above the limit.

PENSION ISSUES

If you are lucky enough to work for an employer who offers a pension, you need to be careful about accepting part-time work from that same employer post-retirement. If, for instance, you downshift into a part-time job with that employer, you might find that your pension benefits are reduced, because your benefits are most likely determined by the combination of salary and years of service. Many pension calculations will weight earnings during the final years of employment higher than other years.

To protect yourself, work with your HR department to figure out if and how your reduced hours and salary will affect your pension benefits. As an alternative to taking the pension hit, you could potentially quit your current job, begin taking your full pension benefits, and return to the company as a contractor.

Another possible pension issue arises if you leave the company, begin taking pension benefits, and then return to work for the same employer. In many cases, the pension plan will not allow you to collect benefits while you are working for the employer providing them. If you cannot afford to work while your benefits are suspended, you will need to figure out if you can work in a contract or freelance capacity—or for another employer.

THE COSTS OF WORKING

We talked extensively in Chapter 8 about the ways that working costs money. Unfortunately, working part-time in retirement can place you in the worst of both worlds in terms of the cost of working and the additional costs of retirement. Because you are still bringing in a paycheck, it can be easy to ignore the work-shaped hole in your budget.

In particular, you will want to make sure that you are not spending too much on the following categories while you are working part-time. Otherwise, you might find it is cheaper not to work at all:

- Gas and car maintenance
- Clothing
- Dining out
- Dry cleaning
- Convenience purchases
- Stress relief
- Professional subscriptions or tools
- Conference costs

Chapter 16 Takeaways

1. Begin your post-retirement job search by figuring out how to match your lifestyle and interests with your search.

2. It's possible to find part-time work that includes benefits. In most cases, you'll have to work at least twenty hours per week to receive the benefits, which may also not match those you received while working full-time.

3. Working part-time will impact your Social Security payments and could affect your pension. Check out these issues before you start work to determine if the extra income you receive from your job will compensate for other expenses you incur by working.

CHAPTER 17

How to Leave a Legacy

WHAT YOU'LL LEARN IN THIS CHAPTER

Everyone hopes to make a mark on the world—and what better way to do that than to leave a financial legacy for your family or for a charity you believe in? Though creating such a legacy can feel out of reach for retirees with limited assets, the truth of the matter is that savvy estate planning can help almost anyone to leave an inheritance. In this chapter, you will learn how to use various financial vehicles—including Roth IRAs, 529 plans, and life insurance policies—to provide an inheritance to your family members even if you retire on a modest budget. Additionally, you will also learn two strategies for providing a legacy to charity while simultaneously securing retirement income for yourself. Whether you are hoping to leave a legacy for family or for charity, by the end of this chapter you will understand the tax implications of each of your estate-planning options.

Using a Roth IRA for Estate Planning

Unlike traditional IRAs, a Roth IRA is funded with after-tax dollars, which means that distributions taken after you have reached age fifty-nine and a half are entirely tax-free. In addition, there is no required minimum distribution for Roth accounts, so you can take these distributions whenever you like—provided that you have reached the age of fifty-nine and a half and you have held the account for at least five years. (Early withdrawals, however, are subject to a 10 percent federal tax penalty, just like with traditional IRAs and 401(k)s.)

What this means for estate planning is that any money you have stashed in a Roth IRA can continue to grow tax-free throughout your lifetime—and can be passed along to a beneficiary without you ever taking a single distribution. Here are the specific allowable rules for inheriting a Roth IRA as a surviving spouse or a non-spousal heir:

1. **Surviving spouse.** The surviving spouse of the Roth IRA account owner may treat the inherited account as his or her own. This means that the spouse may also forgo distributions without penalty—although taking distributions requires the surviving spouse to meet the distribution qualifications (achieving age fifty-nine and a half and having the account open for at least five years). For purposes of estate planning, a married couple can decide that a Roth IRA in one spouse's name could be the planned inheritance for the children. When the account owner passes away, the Roth IRA passes to the spouse, who can then designate the children as the beneficiaries upon his or her death.

2. **Non-spousal heirs.** Whether you name a non-spousal heir as your primary beneficiary or as the beneficiary of a surviving spouse, the IRS requires non-spousal heirs to take minimum distributions. The default rule stipulates that the inherited Roth IRA account must be emptied before the close of the fifth year following the account owner's death. For instance, if the account owner passes away in November 2016, a non-spousal heir would need to empty the account by December 31, 2021.

   However, there is an alternate method for taking minimum distributions, known colloquially as the stretch-out. The stretch-out allows heirs to draw out their minimum required distributions over their expected life spans, which gives the funds even more time to enjoy income-tax-deferred growth.

   It's important to recognize that the IRS takes these required minimum distributions on Roth IRAs very seriously. If you fail to take the required distribution, the IRS levies a 50 percent penalty on the amount that you neglected to take out. For instance, if you had a required minimum distribution of $10,000 from an inherited Roth IRA, failing to take that distribution will mean that you owe the IRS $5,000 when you file your income taxes for the year.

No matter who inherits a Roth IRA, the distributions will be tax-free, making this an excellent way to pass along an inheritance.

If You Have an Estate, You Need a Lawyer

Depending on your specific circumstances, you may find that the options in this chapter could be as simple as filling out a form with an account custodian, or as maddeningly convoluted as figuring out specifics of the U.S. tax code. Even if you have a relatively simple estate, it's a good idea to partner with a lawyer who is an expert in estate planning in order to ensure that your heirs are left with an inheritance, rather than a problem. To find a trusted lawyer in your area, you can check the Martindale-Hubbell database, which allows you to search for attorneys and law firms by practice type, location, and peer rankings. *(www.martindale.com)*

HOW TO DESIGNATE BENEFICIARIES

With any retirement account, you will need to fill out a beneficiary designation form. Without such a form in place, the account will be passed along according to the IRA custodian's default inheritance policy. Generally, that means the IRA will be passed along to the surviving spouse and from there to your estate. Since leaving your Roth IRA to your estate cuts short the tax benefits, this is definitely a situation you want to avoid. In order to ensure that your Roth IRA follows your estate plan, make sure you understand exactly how to designate beneficiaries:

- *Surviving spouse*—Typically, your spouse will be the primary beneficiary of your account. The beneficiary designation form will ask for the percentage share of your primary beneficiary, which will typically be 100 percent. You will also want to name contingent beneficiaries on this form, in case your spouse passes away before you do.
- *Children and grandchildren*—If you hope to leave your Roth IRA to your kids, whether as primary or contingent beneficiaries, you will have to decide how the shares should be divided. For instance, if you have four children, you will likely determine that their shares will each be 25 percent.
- *Per stirpes distributions*—Per stirpes is legalese for passing a deceased beneficiary's share to the next generation, rather than redistributing it to the other named beneficiaries. Let's say that one of your four children passes away. Designating that your distributions are per stirpes (which should be a box you can check on your beneficiary designation form) will pass the deceased child's share of your account on to his children, rather than dividing it among the remaining three siblings.
- *Designating a trust as a beneficiary*—You may designate a trust as your beneficiary for a Roth IRA, which can provide you with more control over how your heirs receive the money after your death. However, the rules regarding trusts as retirement account beneficiaries can be complex, so choosing this option would require the help of a knowledgeable estate attorney.
- *Disclaiming an inheritance*—In some cases, a beneficiary may decide to decline an inheritance from a Roth IRA. This is called "disclaiming," and the law treats those who disclaim their inheritance as if they had died prior to the account owner, leaving the assets to go to the next person in line. You and you family may have an understanding that your primary beneficiary will disclaim the account under certain circumstances so that it can pass to a younger generation who might need it more. It's important to remember, however, that no matter how much you trust your primary beneficiary, you do not know that your wishes for disclaiming the inheritance will be carried out. It might be better to leave money in trust so that you can specify where the funds will go.

President Obama and the Roth IRA

As of this writing, President Obama has made a proposal for the 2016 budget that includes changes to the rules governing Roth IRA accounts. In particular, he has suggested that Roth IRAs require minimum distributions as of age seventy and a half, like their traditional counterparts. In addition, his proposal suggests ending the stretch-out minimum distributions, which currently allows heirs to take distributions based upon life expectancy. Instead, inherited Roth IRAs will have to be emptied within five years of the death of the account holder.

As of right now, these proposals are just that—proposals. As a matter of fact, President Obama has proposed these changes more than once, and nothing has yet been modified in the tax code. However, if you are planning on using a Roth IRA for estate planning, it is a good idea to remember that benefits of this vehicle might change.

OPENING A ROTH IRA

In order to take advantage of the Roth IRA as an estate-planning tool, you need to set one up and start making regular contributions. The only downside to using your Roth IRA for estate planning is the fact that the yearly contribution limit (which is outlined in Table 17-1) encompasses all IRAs you own, meaning you must divide that contribution amount among all IRAs you own, whether they are traditional or Roth. In addition, there are income limits on Roth IRA contributions (also listed in Table 17-1), so some high earners are not able to make contributions to Roth accounts.

TABLE 17-1:
2015 Roth IRA Contribution Limits

FILING STATUS	INCOME LIMIT	CONTRIBUTION LIMIT
Married Filing Jointly	Less than $183,000	$5,500 ($6,500 if over 50)
Married Filing Jointly	$183,001 to $193,000	a reduced amount*
Married Filing Jointly	More than $193,000	0
Single	Less than $116,000	$5,500 ($6,500 if over 50)
Single	$116,001 to $131,000	a reduced amount*
Single	More than $131,000	0

*In order to determine the reduced amount that you may contribute, visit *www.irs.gov/Retirement-Plans/Amount-of-Roth-IRA-Contributions-That-You-Can-Make-For-2015* for the IRS formula for determining the reduction.

If opening a new Roth IRA will not allow you to put away as much money as you would like, you also have the option of converting a traditional IRA into a Roth. However, you will owe ordinary income tax on the amount of money that you convert.

It is possible to pay the taxes owed from your IRA, so that you do not have to pay those taxes out of pocket, but it is generally a better idea to leave your IRA funds where they are so they can continue to grow for you (and your heirs). However, you should remember that the money you convert will be added to your adjusted gross income for the year, potentially pushing you into a higher tax bracket without any real increase in your income to help you pay for the rise in your taxes.

529 Plans and Estate Planning

As we discussed back in Chapter 15, 529 education plans can be an excellent tool for estate planning. That's because assets in a 529 plan are not counted as part of the donor's estate for tax purposes, meaning you can place money outside of your estate by funding such a plan. In addition, there are several other excellent reasons to use a 529 plan as an estate-planning vehicle.

Understanding Estate Taxes

Throughout this chapter, we talk about how different estate-planning vehicles allow you to reduce the size of your taxable estate. As of this writing, reducing the size of your estate is only a problem for the wealthiest Americans. In 2015, the federal estate tax exemption (the amount of money an individual can leave to heirs without having to pay federal taxes on the inheritance) is set at $5.43 million. However, your home state may have a lower estate exemption, meaning you might not owe federal estate taxes but will owe state estate taxes. In addition, the federal estate tax exclusion can be subject to change (it was as low as $1 million just over a decade ago), so it is always a good idea to understand how taxes might affect your estate.

EDUCATION SPECIFIC

If providing an education for your grandchildren (or minor children) is important to you, then using a 529 plan to leave your legacy allows you to specify that your money will be used for education. Other than creating a trust, the 529 plan is the only estate-planning vehicle to ensure that money left to your heirs is spent according to your wishes.

FINANCIAL CONTROL

If your retirement income takes a hit after funding a 529 plan, you can always withdraw some or all of your contribution, although any interest is subject to tax, and you will be liable for the 10 percent penalty for taking a non-qualified distribution.

CONTRIBUTION FLEXIBILITY

Unlike the Roth IRA, which you must either fund while you are employed or fund with a rollover from another retirement account, 529 plans can be created and funded even after you have retired. That means you can set aside some of your retirement income each year to go into the 529 plan, or you can make a single large contribution at a time when you are flush—such as immediately after a career buyout.

Contributions are considered gifts, which means that they need to be below the annual gift exclusion (set at $14,000 per individual recipient for 2015) to avoid triggering the gift tax. However, you may frontload up to five years' worth of gifts ($70,000 per beneficiary of a single donor, $140,000 per beneficiary of a married couple) into a 529 plan without triggering the gift tax, assuming that you make no other gifts to the beneficiary during that five-year period. However, if you make a five-year election of your contribution and pass away before the fifth year, any money allocated for the years after your death are then included in your taxable estate.

Using Life Insurance to Leave a Legacy

Life insurance can be an excellent tool for estate planning. Though life insurance is not necessarily cheap, it can make creating a large inheritance attainable for those on modest budgets, particularly if they enjoy good health. In addition, insurance companies generally approve death benefit claims quickly, meaning life insurance proceeds can be used to pay estate taxes, pay off mortgages, or simply ease financial burdens for your heirs in the aftermath of your death. The proceeds of life insurance are also not considered income for the beneficiary for income tax purposes, making them a tax-free gift to your heirs. Finally, life insurance benefits can avoid both probate (which can be both time-consuming and expensive) and estate taxes, provided you make intelligent designations. Here's what you need to do to make the most of your life insurance legacy:

1. *Name a person as your beneficiary, not your estate.* Making your benefits payable to your estate means the money will be subject to probate and estate taxes.

2. *Name your beneficiary as the owner of your policy.* A common life insurance mistake is to name oneself as the owner of a life insurance policy. If you are listed as both the insured and the owner, then the amount of the benefit is added to your property, making it subject to estate taxes. You can avoid this situation by naming the beneficiary as owner of the policy. However, you must transfer ownership at least three years before your death, or else the life insurance benefits are considered part of your taxable estate.

    There are a couple of important caveats to this strategy, however. First, recognize that transferring ownership means the new owner has all of the rights to the policy, including the right to withdraw the cash value. So it's very important to choose a beneficiary/owner whom you trust. Second, the IRS considers a transfer of ownership of a life insurance policy to be a gift—so if the cash value of the policy is greater than the annual gift exclusion ($14,000 in 2015), then you will owe gift tax on it. However, the gift tax does not need to be paid until your death.

3. *Name an irrevocable life insurance trust as the owner of your policy.* A trust is a financial vehicle where a third party (known as the trustee) holds property placed in trust by the grantor for a beneficiary. The trustee has a fiduciary duty to responsibly handle and invest the money in the trust. An irrevocable life insurance trust is a way to transfer ownership of your policy without giving control of your policy to an individual. You get to determine the terms of the trust, ensuring that your wishes are followed. For instance, your trust could specify that the policy must be kept in effect for your lifetime, which ensures that a new owner of the policy cannot cash it in.

    In order to get full benefit of a life insurance trust, it must be irrevocable, you must choose someone other than yourself as the trustee, and as with a transfer of ownership, you must establish the trust at least three years before your death or the policy proceeds will be included in your taxable estate.

Trusts

Setting up a trust is a good way to make sure that money is available for beneficiaries who might not be able to handle the money on their own. There are any number of other reasons why you might want to set up a trust:

- **Complete control over your assets.** With a trust in place, you can specify exactly when and how your assets will be distributed among your beneficiaries. This is especially helpful for retirees who have children from multiple marriages, since it ensures that the money you intend to go to your children will go straight to them at the time you specify.
- **Protection of your legacy.** If you are concerned about your heirs' spendthrift ways or high debt, a trust can protect the money you intend for them from being seized by their creditors or wasted away through poor money management. You can set up a specific chronology that dictates how much money your heirs will receive at various points in their lives.
- **Avoidance of probate.** While probate is an important part of executing a will, it's not without drawbacks. First—it takes quite a bit of time to complete the probate process. In addition, probate procedures are all public record, meaning anyone can learn more about your estate than you might want them to know. Finally, probate costs can be expensive, averaging anywhere from 6–10 percent of the value of the estate. Setting up a trust allows the assets in trust to pass outside of probate.
- **Reduction of taxes.** Creating a trust can also help families to avoid both gift and estate taxes.

There are several basic types of trust that you may decide to use to distribute your property:

- *Testamentary trust.* This type of trust is outlined in your will and is not created until after you have passed away. The downside to testamentary trusts is that the assets you use to fund it are subject to probate and transfer taxes.
- *Living trusts.* This trust is effective as soon as you open it (which is why it's called "living"), and you can be both the trustee and the grantor. You can choose to make your living trust either revocable—meaning you can change or eliminate the trust altogether at any time—or irrevocable—which means there can be no changes to the trust during your lifetime.
- *Marital or "A" trust.* This kind of vehicle is designed to provide benefits to your surviving spouse while avoiding estate taxes. However, the assets in this sort of trust will be included in the surviving spouse's taxable estate.
- *Bypass or "B" trust.* This is also often called a credit shelter trust. For those retirees with a sizeable estate, a bypass trust can offer you the option of sheltering the money in the trust from estate taxes while still providing your spouse with money to live on. The money in the trust will also bypass the surviving spouse's estate, thereby protecting your joint heirs from estate taxes after you are both gone.
- *Generation-skipping trust.* This kind of trust will allow you to give assets to your grandchildren or great-grandchildren without it having to go to your children first. That can help protect the assets from both potential mismanagement and your children's estate taxes.
- *Qualified terminable interest property (QTIP) trust.* This kind of trust is common in blended families, as it provides a surviving spouse with income during his/her life, but the assets will go to additional beneficiaries after the death of the surviving spouse.

Trusts can help you to solve otherwise difficult estate-planning dilemmas, but they are not necessarily for everyone. Depending on the complexity of your trust, it can cost up to several thousand dollars for your attorney to draw up your trust. But if controlling your financial legacy from the grave is important to you, a trust is the best way to go.

Leaving a Legacy to Your Favorite Charity

Creating an inheritance for your family is not the only way to leave a financial legacy. You can also make sure that the charities you care deeply about benefit from your generosity, even if you don't enjoy Rockefeller levels of wealth. In fact, two types of charitable giving can benefit your favorite causes while also generating a retirement income for you, making it a win-win.

CHARITABLE GIFT ANNUITY

Like a traditional annuity purchased through an insurance company, a charitable gift annuity is a contract under which you pay a charity a lump sum and get in return a fixed monthly payment for life. You can fund a gift annuity with cash, marketable securities, or other assets.

The charity invests the gift, and it becomes part of the charity's assets. The annuity is backed by the entirety of the charity's assets (not just the gift), which means annuity payments are guaranteed no matter what happens to the invested gift. At the time of your death, the charity gets to keep the principal—which could potentially still be intact depending on how the institution has managed its investments.

When you take advantage of such a charitable giving plan, you not only get to count on an annuity payment for life, but you also get to consider the initial donation as a tax deduction in the year that you make the gift, and at least a portion of your annuity payments are treated as a partial tax-free return of your gift—although you will owe regular income tax on the rest of each annuity payment.

Charitable gift annuities are particularly appealing for investors who have taxable investments that enjoyed exceptional growth. Under normal circumstances, if you were to sell those investments, the sale would trigger the capital gains tax, which in most cases will eat up 15 percent of that growth (as of 2015). However, by gifting the investment to a charity (which is tax exempt), the institution is able to take advantage of the full value of the investment while you get to enjoy a guaranteed income stream for life. In addition, you will avoid both estate and gift taxes on the property used for the annuity.

For more information about charitable gift annuities and the charities that utilize them, check out the American Council on Gift Annuities (*www.acga-web.org*).

CHARITABLE REMAINDER TRUST

Like the charitable gift annuity, a charitable remainder trust allows you to give a gift to a charity while providing yourself with guaranteed income for life. However, this vehicle is a trust that you must set up with the help of a financial planner and/or an attorney.

To create such a trust, you gift a lump sum (or an investment or other assets) to a trust, the ultimate beneficiary of which is your favorite charity. In effect, this transfers ownership of the assets from you to the charity. The charity will receive whatever principal remains in the trust at the time of your death.

When you create the trust, you will determine the specific terms regarding how the funds will be invested and how much income will be paid out to you. There are two types of charitable remainder trusts: annuity trusts and unitrusts. Annuity trusts pay out a fixed amount that you set at the time you put the trust in place, while unitrusts make regular payments based on a percentage of the value of the trust. Unitrusts allow you to enjoy periods of growth, but you also see your income go down with market downturns. In addition, annuity trusts are "closed," meaning you cannot add any property or assets to such a trust, while unitrusts allow you to add more assets at any time.

As with a charitable gift annuity, using such a trust can help you to avoid paying capital gains taxes on appreciated assets, since charities are tax exempt. You can also claim an income tax deduction on your initial gift, although the calculation for determining the deduction is incredibly complex, since it is based upon your life expectancy, the projected value of the trust at the time of transfer to the charity (i.e., your death), and the income you are expected over your lifetime. As with the charitable gift annuity, the funds in your charitable remainder trust do not generate estate or gift taxes.

Unlike the charitable gift annuity, you still have control over the assets in a charitable remainder trust. You (along with your financial planner) get to decide how the money is invested, not the charity.

Chapter 17 Takeaways

1. Leaving a legacy is largely a matter of good estate planning. There are a number of instruments with which to do this, most prominently a Roth IRA.

2. You can also use a 529 plan to leave an education legacy. This method also gives you more control over how the money will be allocated.

3. Another tool to use in estate planning is life insurance. This can help you leave a large inheritance on a modest budget.

4. If you're concerned that beneficiaries might not be able to handle the money you leave to them, consider setting up a trust.

5. Besides leaving money to your family, you can make a bequest to a charity: either a charitable gift annuity or a charitable remainder trust.

Conclusion

On its surface, retirement planning seems to be all about boring financial decisions: how much to invest in what kinds of assets, how much you will owe in taxes, how much to plan for this expense vs. that expense, how to calculate benefits, and so on. These are certainly the topics that any layperson will need the help of a well-written guide or a trusted adviser to navigate. But retirement planning is much more than just dollars and cents; it's your future. Forgetting that fact and focusing on the dry-as-sawdust topics makes many people avoid doing the work they need to do in order to prepare for their retirement.

At its heart, retirement planning (and all financial planning) seeks to help you live your life the way you want to. It is about giving you the freedom to follow your passions, shape your path, and choose your retirement. Retirement planning, in a nutshell, is the practical application of dreaming big and knowing yourself.

For that reason, planning a retirement is highly individual.

Only *you* know exactly what is keeping you from saving and investing money for your future. Only *you* recognize which outside influences you are most susceptible to. Only *you* understand your personal risk factors. Only *you* know which values are most important to you in achieving a fulfilling retirement. And only *you* can determine what you want your second act to look like on a daily, weekly, monthly, and yearly basis.

I can't tell you exactly what will work for your journey or what your journey will look like—and neither can any other retirement expert. That is why this book gives you the tools you need to better understand the personal, practical, emotional, and behavioral barriers standing in the way of the retirement of your dreams.

It's now up to you to remove those barriers, make your big plans, and start along the path to your retirement adventure.

And there's nothing boring about that.

Bibliography

Atanasova, Vasilka. "Moving Rates Average—Locally and Long Distance." My Moving Reviews. December 16, 2011. *www.mymovingreviews.com/move/moving-rates-average.*

"Avoid Moving Scams. Protect Your Move." U.S. Department of Transportation Federal Motor Carrier Safety Administration Household Goods Program. *www.protectyourmove.gov.*

Baumeister, Roy F., and John Tierney. *Willpower: Rediscovering the Greatest Human Strength.* New York: Penguin Books, 2012.

Birken, Emily Guy. "3 Outdated Retirement 'Rules' You Should Ignore." *MoneyNing.* July 21, 2014. *http://moneyning.com/retirement/3-outdated-retirement-rules-you-should-ignore.*

Birken, Emily Guy. *The 5 Years Before You Retire: Retirement Planning When You Need It the Most.* Avon, MA: Adams Media, 2014.

Birken, Emily Guy. "Best Part-Time Jobs with Benefits—Updated for the 2014 Implementation of Obamacare." *PT Money.* June 23, 2014. *http://ptmoney.com/the-ten-best-part-time-jobs-with-benefits.*

Block, Sandra. "How to Retire Abroad." *Kiplinger.* August, 2013. *http://www.kiplinger.com/article/retirement/T037-C000-S002-how-to-retire-abroad.html.*

Brandon, Emily. "How to Reduce Taxes on Your Social Security Payments." *US News & World Report*. February 9, 2015. *http://money.usnews.com/money/retirement/articles/2015/02/09/how-to-reduce-taxes-on-your-social-security-payments*.

Brandon, Emily. "Taxes to Watch Out for in Retirement." *US News & World Report*. August 4, 2014. *http://money.usnews.com/money/retirement/articles/2014/08/04/taxes-to-watch-out-for-in-retirement*.

"Can I Retire Young?" Early Retirement Extreme. July 4, 2014. *http://www.earlyretirementextreme.com/can-i-retire-young.html*.

"Caregiving Resource Center: The Downsizing Dilemma, Moving Out." AARP. September, 2010. *www.aarp.org/relationships/caregiving-resource-center/info-09-2010/ho_the_downsizing_dilemma.1.html*.

Coombes, Andrea. How to Retire Early—35 Years Early." MarketWatch. December 26, 2014. *www.marketwatch.com/story/how-to-retire-early-35-years-early-2014-01-17*.

Crosby, Daniel. "The Ten Commandments of Investor Behavior." Lecture, FinCon14, New Orleans, LA, September 19, 2014.

Damodaran, Aswath. "Annual Returns on Stock, T.Bonds and T.Bills: 1928–Current." Historical Returns. Updated January 5, 2015. *http://pages.stern.nyu.edu/~adamodar/New_Home_Page/datafile/histretSP.html*.

Drenkard, Scott. "State and Local Sales Tax Rates in 2014." Tax Foundation. March 18, 2014. *http://taxfoundation.org/article/state-and-local-sales-tax-rates-2014*.

Dunn, Nora. "Travel for a Living on Less Than $14,000 Per Year." *I Will Teach You to Be Rich*. May 18, 2009. *www.iwillteachyoutoberich.com/blog/how-to-travel-cheap*.

Duprey, Rich. "Profit from Market Timing." The Motley Fool. January 23, 2007. *www.fool.com/investing/general/2007/01/23/profit-from-market-timing.aspx*.

Dynarski, Susan, and Judith Scott-Clayton. "There Is a Simpler Way for Students to Apply for Financial Aid." *New York Times*, June 20, 2014. *www.nytimes.com/2014/06/21/upshot/a-simple-way-to-help-financial-aid-do-its-job.html?abt=0002&abg=0&_r=0*.

Ebeling, Ashlea. "Four Ways to Beat High Health Care Costs; Fidelity Says Recent Retirees Need $220,000!" *Forbes*. May 15, 2013. *www.forbes.com/sites/ashleaebeling/2013/05/15/four-ways-to-beat-high-health-care-costs-fidelity-says-recent-retirees-need-220000*.

"Education Credits—AOTC and LLC." IRS. Updated December 11, 2014. *www.irs.gov/Individuals/Education-Credits-AOTC-LLC*.

Eisenberg, Richard. "How to Retire Overseas on Under $25,000 a Year." *Forbes*. March 27, 2014. *www.forbes.com/sites/nextavenue/2014/03/27/how-to-retire-overseas-on-under-25000-a-year*.

Ekerdt, David J., and Lindsey A. Baker. "The Material Convoy after Age 50." *Journals of Gerontology Psychological Sciences & Social Sciences Series B* 69, no. 3 (2014): 442–50. *http://psychsocgerontology.oxfordjournals.org/content/69/3/442*.

Epperson, Sharon. "Most of Us Making 'Fair' or 'No' Progress in Savings." CNBC. February 25, 2014. *www.cnbc.com/id/101441422#*.

Friedberg, Leora, Wenliang Hou, Wei Sun, and Anthony Webb. "Long-Term Care: How Big a Risk?" Center for Retirement Research at Boston College, Number 14–18 (November 2014): 1–11. *http://crr.bc.edu/wp-content/uploads/2014/11/IB_14-18_508_rev.pdf*.

Gailliot, Matthew T., and Roy F. Baumeister. "The Physiology of Willpower: Linking Blood Glucose to Self-Control." *Personality and Social Psychology Review* 11, no. 4 (2007). 303–27.

"Genworth 2014 Cost of Care Survey." Genworth. 2014. *www.genworth.com/dam/Americas/US/PDFs/Consumer/corporate/131168-032514-Executive-Summary-nonsecure.pdf*.

Greene, Kelly. "Continuing-Care Retirement Communities: Weighing the Risks." *Wall Street Journal*. August 10, 2010. *www.wsj.com/articles/SB100014 24052748704499604575407290112356422*.

Harrington, Judith B., and Stanley J. Steinberg. *The Everything® Retirement Planning Book: A Complete Guide to Managing Your Investments, Securing Your Future, and Enjoying Life to the Fullest*. Avon, MA: Adams Media, 2007.

Harvey, John T. "Social Security Cannot Go Bankrupt." *Forbes*. August 14, 2014. *www.forbes.com/sites/johntharvey/2014/08/14/ social-security-cannot-go-bankrupt*.

Haskins, Suzan, and Dan Precher. *The International Living Guide to Retiring Overseas on a Budget: How to Live Well on $25,000 a Year*. 1st ed. New York: Wiley, 2014.

Hebeler, Henry K. 2013. "Free Replacement Budgeting" Analyze Now. *www.analyzenow.com/Free%20Programs/free_programs.htm*.

Horner, Elizabeth Mokyr, "Subjective Well-Being and Retirement: Analysis and Policy Recommendations." *Journal of Happiness Studies* (2012): DOI 10.1007/s10902-012-9399-2.

"How Much Do You Need to Retire?" Fidelity Investments. January 30, 2014. *www.fidelity.com/viewpoints/retirement/8X-retirement-savings*.

"Journey to Healthy Aging: Planning for Travel in Retirement." *Transamerica Center for Retirement Studies*, 2013. *www.transamericacenter.org/docs/default-source/resources/travel-survey/tcrs2013_sr_travel_and_aging.pdf*.

Kelly, Caitlin. "Choosing to Live Abroad in Retirement." *New York Times*. November 14, 2014. *www.nytimes.com/2014/11/15/your-money/choosing-to-live-abroad-in-retirement.html*.

Klontz, Bradley T. Interview by author. Phone interview. Lafayette, IN, September 22, 2014.

Klontz, Bradley T., "Klontz Money Script Inventory," *Kiplinger.* August 2012.

Klontz, Bradley T., and Sonya L. Britt. "How Clients' Money Scripts Predict Their Financial Behaviors." *Journal of Financial Planning* 25, no. 11 (2012). *www.onefpa.org/journal/Pages/How Clients' Money Scripts Predict Their Financial Behaviors.aspx.*

Laise, Eleanor. "Risks and Rewards of Moving to a CCRC." *Kiplinger.* January 1, 2013. *www.kiplinger.com/article/retirement/T037-C000-S000-risks-and-rewards-of-moving-to-a-ccrc.html.*

Lambert, Craig. "The Marketplace of Perceptions." *Harvard Magazine*, March-April, 2006. *http://harvardmagazine.com/2006/03/the-marketplace-of-perce.html.*

Landes, Luke. "Retirement Savings Goals Should Be Based on Expenses Not Income." *Forbes.* September 17, 2012. *www.forbes.com/sites/moneybuilder/2012/09/17/retirement-savings-goals-should-be-based-on-expenses-not-income.*

Layton, Deborah S. *The Everything® Wills & Estate Planning Book: Professional Advice to Safeguard Your Assets and Provide Security for Your Family.* 2nd ed. Avon, MA: Adams Media, 2009.

Leybovich, Ilya. "Health Benefits of Working after Retirement." Industry News. October 22, 2009. *http://news.thomasnet.com/imt/2009/10/22/physical-mental-health-benefits-of-working-beyond-retirement-age.*

MacDonald, Jay. "Steps to a Successful Encore Career" Bankrate.com. *www.bankrate.com/finance/jobs-careers/steps-to-successful-encore-career-1.aspx#ixzz3T2ZeRZJ5.*

Morath, Eric. "Where Are the U.S.'s Millionaires?" *Wall Street Journal.* January 16, 2014. *http://blogs.wsj.com/economics/2014/01/16/where-are-the-u-s-s-millionaires/?mod=WSJ_hps_MIDDLENexttoWhatsNewsForth.*

National Reverse Mortgage Lenders Association. "Application, Fees, and Disclosures." Your Reverse Mortgage Road Map. *www.reversemortgage.org/ YourRoadmap/4ApplicationFeesDisclosures.aspx*.

Olson, Jeff, and John David Mann. *The Slight Edge: Turning Simple Disciplines into Massive Success and Happiness*. 8th Anniversary ed. Austin, TX: Greenleaf Book Group Press, 2013.

Park, Denise C., Jennifer Lodi-Smith, Linda Drew, Sara Haber, Andrew Hebrank, Gerard N. Bischof, and Whitley Aamodt. "The Impact of Sustained Engagement on Cognitive Function in Older Adults." *Psychological Science* 25, no. 1 (2013): 103–12. *http://pss.sagepub.com/ content/25/1/103*.

Powell, Robert. "Most Tax-Friendly States for Retirees." MarketWatch. January 31, 2014. *www.marketwatch.com/story/most-tax-friendly-states-for-retirees-2014-01-31*.

Pychyl, Timothy A. "Self-Regulation Failure (Part 3): What's Motivation Got to Do with It?" *Psychology Today*, February 27, 2009. *www.psychologytoday.com/ blog/dont-delay/200902/self-regulation-failure-part-3-whats-motivation-got-do-it*.

Reno, Virginia P., and Joni Lavery. "Can We Afford Social Security When Baby Boomers Retire?" *Social Security Brief* No. 22 (May 2006): 1–12. *www.nasi.org/sites/default/files/research/SS_Brief_022.pdf*.

"Rent an RV Before You Buy One (Or, Instead of Buying One)." RVing. May 18, 2007. *http://rv-roadtrips.thefuntimesguide.com/2007/05/rent_an_rv_motorhome.php*.

"Retiree Health Costs Hold Steady." Fidelity. June 11, 2014. *www.fidelity.com/ viewpoints/retirement/retirees-medical-expenses*.

Robinson, Lawrence, Joanna Saisan, and Doug Russell. "Independent Living for Seniors: Choosing a Retirement Home or Retirement Facility." HelpGuide.org. Updated February, 2015. *www.helpguide.org/articles/senior-housing/independent-living-for-seniors.htm#costs*.

Rosenbloom, Stephanie. "What a Great Trip! And I'm Not Even There Yet." *New York Times*. May 10, 2014. *www.nytimes.com/2014/05/11/travel/what-a-great-trip-and-im-not-even-there-yet.html*.

Sethi, Ramit. "Barriers Are Your Enemy." *I Will Teach You to Be Rich*. October 17, 2005. *www.iwillteachyoutoberich.com/blog/barriers-are-your-enemy*.

Sethi, Ramit. "The Psychology of Passive Barriers: Why Your Friends Don't Save Money, Eat Healthier, or Clean Their Garages." *Get Rich Slowly*. October 9, 2009. *www.getrichslowly.org/blog/2009/03/17/the-psychology-of-passive-barriers-why-your-friends-dont-save-money-eat-healthier-or-clean-their-garages*.

Sheedy, Rachel L. "Retirees, Watch Out for the State Tax Bite." *Kiplinger*. October, 2014. *www.kiplinger.com/article/retirement/T055-C000-S004-retirees-watch-out-for-the-state-tax-bite.html*.

"Social Security Basic Facts." Social Security Administration. April 2, 2014. *www.ssa.gov/news/press/basicfact.html*.

Span, Paula. "Paying Taxes on Social Security Benefits." *New York Times*. September 13, 2010. *http://newoldage.blogs.nytimes.com/2010/09/13/paying-taxes-on-social-security-benefits/?_r=0*.

"Stanford Marshmallow Experiment." Wikipedia. Accessed September 10, 2014. *http://en.wikipedia.org/wiki/Stanford_marshmallow_experiment*.

Su, Tina. "Life on Purpose: 15 Questions to Discover Your Personal Mission." Think Simple Now. *http://thinksimplenow.com/happiness/life-on-purpose-15-questions-to-discover-your-personal-mission*.

Szalavitz, Maia. "Self-Disciplined People Are Happier (and Not As Deprived As You Think)." *Time*, June 24, 2013.

"Tax Benefits for Education: Information Center." IRS. Updated January 15, 2015. *www.irs.gov/uac/Tax-Benefits-for-Education:-Information-Center*.

Tetlock, Philip E. *Expert Political Judgment: How Good Is It? How Can We Know?* Princeton, N.J.: Princeton University Press, 2005.

Tresidder, Todd. "5 Ways to Reduce Retirement Savings Needs by $300,000 (or More!)" Financial Mentor. *http://financialmentor.com/free-articles/ retirement-planning/how-much-to-retire/5-ways-to-reduce.*

"U.S. Citizens and Resident Aliens Abroad." IRS. Updated December 5, 2014. *www.irs.gov/Individuals/International-Taxpayers/U.S.-Citizens-and-Resident-Aliens-Abroad.*

Vernon, Steve. "More People Are Delaying Social Security Benefits." CBS MoneyWatch. April 8, 2014. *www.cbsnews.com/news/ more-people-are-delaying-social-security-benefits.*

Wang, Penelope. "Here's a New Reason to Think Twice Before Buying Long-Term Care Insurance." *Money.* November 11, 2014. *http://time.com/ money/3578466/long-term-care-insurance-study.*

Wilkinson, David. "Action Bias in Decision Making & Problem Solving." *Ambiguity Advantage.* February 21, 2008. *http://ambiguityadvantage.blogspot.com/2008/02/ action-bias-in-decision-making-problem.html.*

Worldwide ERC. "Facts & Statistics: U.S. Domestic Transfers: Relocation Statistics," 2013. *www.worldwideerc.org/resources/research/pages/facts-and- statistics.aspx.*

Zemelman, I.J. "U.S. Taxes While Living Abroad FAQ." American Citizens Abroad: The Voice of Americans Overseas. Updated March 16, 2015. *https://americansabroad.org/issues/taxation/us-taxes-while-living-abroad-faq.*

Index

A

AARP Health Expense
  Calculator, 87
absentee voting, 154
action bias, 43–44
active barriers, 26–27
Aerotek, 216
affect heuristic, 39–40
Affordable Care Act, 156,
  189–91
age discrimination, 200–201
Airbnb, 167
airline tickets, 165–66
American Opportunity Tax
  Credit (AOTC), 209–10
annual living expenses, 177
asset allocation
  bucket method of, 69–71
  rebalancing, 45–46, 71
assets, cash equivalent, 70
assisted living facilities, 138
"A" trust, 231

audit classes, 209

B

baby boomers, 76
banking, living abroad and,
  150–52, 154–55
beneficiaries
  designating, 223–25
  for life insurance, 229
benevolent funds, 142
biking, 178
blogging, 163–64
bonds, 38
"B" trust, 231
bucket method, 69–71
budgeting
  during retirement, 103–12
  for travel, 162
Buffett, Warren, 39
buy-and-hold strategy, 44, 45
bypass trust, 231

C

Café Press, 164
career changes, 195–203
car expenses, 107, 178
cash equivalent assets, 70
CCRCs. *See* continuing care retirement communities (CCRCs)
charitable donations, 33, 232–34
charitable gift annuity, 232–33
charitable remainder trust, 233–34
Chico's FAS, 216
children. *See also* family belongings of, 129
citizenship, living abroad and, 154–55
college education, 205–12, 227
compound interest, 104–5, 184
Consumer Price Index (CPI), 192
consumption, 177–78
Container Store, 216
continuing care retirement communities (CCRCs), 138–44
Costco, 217
cost of living, 133, 148–50
Cost Plus World Market, 217
Couch Surfing, 167

Coursera, 211
Covey, Stephen, 49
crafts, selling, 164
Cramer, Jim, 42
credit card miles, 166
credit cards, barriers to use of, 32, 34–35
credit shelter trust, 231
Crosby, Daniel, 39, 40, 41, 43, 44, 46
cruises
last minute, 168
repositioning, 166

D

distraction, 21
doctors, 122–23, 155
dog-sitting/walking, 164
dotcom bubble, 39
downsizing, 119, 127–30, 169
dream retirement, 50–56

E

early retirement, 175–94
accessing income in, 184–87
affording, 175–84
amount needed for, 179–84
common headaches in, 187–94
family considerations, 193–94

healthcare issues and, 188–91

inflation and, 192–93

Early Retirement Extreme, 176

education, 205–12, 227

educational travel, 168

Edward M. Kennedy Serve America Act, 209

ego depletion, 21, 22

emotions, investment decisions and, 38–40

employer-provided health benefits, 188–89, 215–18

employment
part-time, 213–20
second careers, 195–203
self-employment, 197

encore careers, 195–203

entertainment, living abroad and, 149

entrepreneurship, 197

estate planning
529 plans and, 208, 226–28
charitable donations and, 232–34
lawyers for, 223
life insurance for, 228–30
Roth IRA for, 221–26
trusts and, 230–32

estate taxes, 227, 229, 230, 231

Etsy, 164

exercise, 124

expenses
annual living, 177
car, 107, 178
education, 206
healthcare, 86–87
multiplier, 181
reducing your, 178–79, 182–84
replacement, 109–11
retirement, 66–68, 86–87, 105–6, 109, 180–84
work-related, 219

expert predictions, 42–43

F

family
dynamics, 135
early retirement and, 193–94
moving closer to, 127–37
moving in with, 135
relationships with, 134

fear, 38–39

Federal Motor Carrier Safety Administration (FMCSA), 131

fee-for-service contracts, 140

55+ retirement communities, 137–38

finances, living abroad and, 150–52

financial aid, 25–26

financial beliefs, 13–23

Financial Crimes Enforcement Network (FinCEN) Form 114, 153

financial decisions, fear-based, 35

529 plans, 205–8, 226–28

5/3 Bank, 217

The Five Whys, 27–32

Fixed Amortization method, 186

Fixed Annuitization method, 186–87

Flexible Spending Accounts, 87–88

floor plans, 128–29

food, living abroad and, 149

forecasting, 42–43

Foreign Account Tax Compliance Act, 151

foreign bank accounts, 150–52, 154–55

foreign earned income, 153

foreign language, learning, 157

foreign taxes, 153

Form 1040, 152

Form 8938, 152

401(k), 184, 185, 202, 206, 207

4 percent withdrawal rule, 68–71

Free Application for Federal Student Aid (FAFSA), 25–26

free education online, 211

freelance work, 163, 214

Frugal Travel Guy, 166

fulfillment, 123–24

future predictions, 42–43

G

generation-skipping trust, 231

gift taxes, 229, 230

Global Freeloaders, 167

goal setting, 49–60, 198

greed, 38–39

Greenspan, Alan, 39

guaranteed income, 104

guilt, 16

H

happiness, 123, 172, 179

healthcare
costs, 86–87
early retirement and, 188–91
employer-provided health benefits, 188–89, 215–18
home, 94
hospital care, 92–93

issues to consider, 119–23
living abroad and, 155–56
long-term care insurance,
  96–98
Medicare, 85–86, 91–96
myths about, 85–99
part-time jobs and, 215–18
saving for, 87–90
healthcare providers, 122–23
health insurance, 85–98, 156,
  170–71, 188–91. *See also*
  Medicare
Health Insurance Marketplace,
  190–91
Health Savings Accounts
  (HSAs), 87–89
heirlooms, 129
Help Exchange, 167
high-deductible health plan
  (HDHP), 88–89
home healthcare, 94
hospice care, 94–95
hospital care, 92–93
hospitality exchanges, 167
House Carers, 167
housing issues
  downsizing, 119, 127–30
  overseas retirement and, 148
  in retirement, 112–19

I
income
  accessing retirement, 184–87
  foreign earned, 153
  guaranteed, 104
  investment, 104–5
  myths, 63–72
  sources of retirement, 163–
    64
  systematic withdrawal and,
    68–71
income taxes, 132, 152–54
independent living
  communities, 138
index funds, 43
individual retirement accounts
  (IRAs)
  accessing early, 184–87
  contributions to, 202
  limits on, 90
  Roth, 90, 207, 221–26
inflation, 41, 67, 98, 192–93
inheritance. *See also* estate
  planning
  disclaiming, 224
insurance
  healthcare, 85–98, 156,
    170–71
  life, 228–30
  long-term care insurance,
    96–98

for RVs, 170
travel, 171–72
interest, compound, 104–5,
184
investment decisions, 37–47
emotions and, 38–40
long-term, 46
rational, 40–46
investments
4 percent withdrawal rule
and, 68–71
bonds, 38
income from, 104–5
inflation and, 193
mutual funds, 38
rebalancing, 45
return on, 176–77
stocks, 38, 40
vehicles for, 38
IRAs. *See* individual retirement
accounts (IRAs)

J
job seekers, 200–201
Jobs for the Older and Bolder,
215

K
Khan Academy, 211
Klontz, Bradley, 14, 18

Klontz Money Script Inventory,
16–17

L
legacy planning, 221–34
life care contracts, 140
life insurance, 228–30
Lifetime Learning Credit (LLC),
210
LinkedIn, 200
living abroad, 147–60
choosing location for, 158–
59
citizenship and entitlements,
154–55
costs of, 147–50, 151
exit strategy, 158
handling finances while,
150–52
healthcare and, 155–56
taxes and, 152–54
transitioning to, 157–58
living trusts, 231
long-term care, 96
long-term care insurance, 96–98
Lowe's, 217

M
maintenance, housing, 117–19
marital trust, 231
market downturns, 69

market timing, 44

marshmallow experiment, 21

media, 42

Medicaid, 97

Medicare

  doctors who accept, 122–23

  enrollment in, 119–22

  geographical limits of,
    170–71

  living abroad and, 155

  myths about, 85–86, 91–96

  Part A coverage, 91–95,
    120–22

  Part B coverage, 95–96,
    120–22

Medicare Advantage Plan, 171

memories, writing down,
  129–30

mentors, 198

Minimum Distribution
  method, 185–86

Mischel, Walter, 21

mobility issues, 113, 117–19

modified contracts, 140

money

  attitude toward, 13–23

  guilt, 16

money avoidance, 15, 33

money scripts

  combatting with small
    barriers, 33–35

  determining your, 16–19

  retirement path and, 19–20

  types of, 14–18

  understanding, 14

money status, 15, 34–35

money vigilance, 15–16, 35

money worship, 15, 34–35

mortgages

  paying off pre-retirement, 112

  reverse, 113–17

motivation, 22–23

moving

  to be closer to family, 127–37

  cost of living and, 133

  downsizing, 119, 127–30

  in with family, 135

  financial considerations of,
    130–33

  managing expectations for,
    134

  into retirement community,
    137–46

  taxes and, 132–33

moving companies, 131–32

Mr. Money Mustache (MMM),
  178–79

multigenerational households,
  135

mutual funds, 38

mystery shopping, 164

myths. *See* retirement myths

N

NerdWallet, 166

nest egg
   amount needed for, 64–68
   return on, 176–77
   withdrawal strategies, 68–71
non-spousal heirs, 222–23, 224
nursing home costs, 96

O

Olson, Jeff, 40
online education, 211
organization, 130
overseas retirement, 147–60
   choosing location for, 158–
      59
   citizenship and entitlements,
      154–55
   costs of, 147–50, 151
   exit strategy, 158
   handling finances, 150–52
   healthcare and, 155–56
   taxes and, 152–54
   transitions, 157–58

P

part-time work, 213–20
passive barriers, 27
Patriot Act, 152
pensions, 218–19
per stirpes distributions, 224

pet sitting/walking, 164
"Plan B" retirement, 56–59
portfolio rebalancing, 45–46,
   71
possessions, purging, 128–30
post-retirement education,
   205–12
prescription drugs, 96
probate, 230
procrastination, 26–32
property taxes, 132
psychological issues, 123–24
psychology, of money, 13–23
purchases, twenty-four-hour
   rule for, 34
Pychyl, Timothy, 22

Q

qualified terminable interest
   property (QTIP) trust, 231

R

rational investing, 40–46
rebalancing, 45–46, 71
recreational vehicles (RVs),
   168–70
REI, 217
relocation costs, 130–33. *See
   also* moving
replacement expenses, 109–11
repositioning cruises, 166

required minimum
  distributions (RMDs), 202,
  221, 222–23, 225
resumé, 200
retirement
  abroad, 147–60
  budgeting in, 103–12
  changing careers in, 195–
    203
  early, 175–94
  education in, 205–12
  healthcare issues in, 119–23
  housing issues in, 112–19
  inflation and, 192–93
  managing expectations in,
    134
  part-ime work in, 213–20
  psychological issues in,
    123–24
  savings from, 107–9
  traveling during, 161–73
retirement accounts, 90, 184–
  87, 202, 221–26
Retirement Charming, 59–60
retirement communities
  continuing care retirement
    communities (CCRCs),
    138–44
  finding right fit, 145–46
  types of, 137–39
retirement dreams, 50–56

retirement expenses, 66–68,
  86–87, 105–6, 109, 180–84
Retirement Income Calculator,
  104–5
retirement myths
  about healthcare, 85–99
  about income, 63–72
  about Medicare, 91–96
  about Social Security, 73–84
  myths about, 85–86
retirement path
  money scripts and, 19–20
  small barriers and, 26–36
retirement planning
  barriers to, 25–36
  goal setting and, 49–60
  motivation for, 22–23
retirement savings
  amount needed for, 64–68
  automatic transfers for, 33
  return on, 176–77
  withdrawal strategies, 68–71
reverse mortgages, 113–17
risk, 40–41
risk tolerance, 41–42, 46
Road Scholar, 168
Roth IRA, 90, 207, 221–26
Rule of 55, 184–85

S

sales tax, 132–33

savings
  amount needed in, 64–68
  education, 205–8
  healthcare, 87–90
  retirement, 107–9
  systematic withdrawal from, 68–71

second careers, 195–203

self-discipline, 20–23

self-employment, 197

self-worth, 15

senior discounts, 165

Servas, 167

Sethi, Ramit, 26–27, 29

72(t) Early Distribution Rule, 184–87

skilled nursing facility care, 93–94

skills, learning new, 124

small barriers, 25–36

SMART goals, 198

social media, 200

Social Security
  calculation of benefits for, 77–79
  financial stability of, 74–75
  living abroad and, 154–55
  myths about, 73–84
  part-time work and, 218
  revenue streams of, 75–76
  second careers and, 201–2
  taxation, 77, 79–83, 133, 202
  worker-to-retiree ratio and, 76

spending, ways to reduce, 178–79, 182–84

Spread Shirt, 164

Starbucks, 218

stock market
  downturns in, 69
  returns, 43, 69
  timing, 44

stock photography sites, 164

stocks, 38, 40

Substantially Equal Periodic Payments (SEPP), 185

Summary Plan Description (SPD), 188–89

surviving spouses, 222, 224

systematic withdrawal, 68–71

T

tax credits, for education, 209–10

taxes
  CCRCs and, 144
  estate, 227, 229, 230, 231
  foreign, 153
  gift, 229, 230
  income, 132, 152–54

living abroad and, 149, 152–54

moving and, 132–33

property, 132

sales, 132–33

on Social Security, 77, 79–83, 133, 202

trusts and, 230

television, 179

temptations, 20–21, 22

testamentary trust, 231

Tetlock, Philip, 42

Tierney, John, 21

transportation

air, 165–66

living abroad and, 149

reducing costs of, 178

saving on, 165–66

travel

accommodations, 166–67

affordable, 161–62

budgeting for, 162

educational, 168

getting the most out of, 172–73

insurance, 171–72

off-season, 165

package deals, 167–68

planning ahead for, 162–64

reducing costs of, 164–68

during retirement, 161–73

RVs, 168–70

transportation, 165–66

Treasure Inflation Protected Securities (TIPS), 193

trusts, 224, 229–32, 233–34

T-shirt design, 164

tuition assistance, 209

tuition deduction, 210

tutoring, 164

U

U.S. address, 152

utilities, 148

V

Vacation Rentals By Owner, 167

values, 52–54

values-driven retirement, 54–56

volatility, 40–41

volunteering, 124, 196

W

waiver-of-premium benefit, 98

willpower, 20–21

withdrawal strategies, 68–71

Workamper News, 215

work-related expenses, 219

worst-case scenarios, 23, 57

writing, freelance, 163

About the Author

Emily Guy Birken is a former educator and a respected personal finance blogger. Her background in education allows her to make complex financial topics relatable and easily understood by the layperson. Her work has appeared on the sites PTMoney, Wise Bread, MoneyNing, Huffington Post, and Business Insider, as well as Kiplinger's, MSN Money, and *New York Times* online. She has also appeared on the Wisconsin Public Radio program *Central Time* hosted by Rob Ferrett and on *The Chad Slagle Show* on the CBS affiliate KMOV in St. Louis.

Emily has a Bachelor's Degree in English with an emphasis in creative writing from Kenyon College, and a Master's Degree in Education from The Ohio State University. She currently lives in Lafayette, Indiana, with her husband Jayme, a mechanical engineer, and her two sons, Ari and James.